JUSTINIAN

❖

THE DIGEST OF ROMAN LAW

THEFT, RAPINE, DAMAGE AND INSULT

❖

TRANSLATED BY
C. F. KOLBERT

PENGUIN BOOKS

Published by the Penguin Group
Penguin Books Ltd, 80 Strand, London WC2R 0RL, England
Penguin Putnam Inc., 375 Hudson Street, New York, New York 10014, USA
Penguin Books Australia Ltd, 250 Camberwell Road, Camberwell, Victoria 3124, Australia
Penguin Books Canada Ltd, 10 Alcorn Avenue, Toronto, Ontario, Canada M4V 3B2
Penguin Books India (P) Ltd, 11 Community Centre, Panchsheel Park, New Delhi – 110 017, India
Penguin Books (NZ) Ltd, Cnr Rosedale and Airborne Roads, Albany, Auckland, New Zealand
Penguin Books (South Africa) (Pty) Ltd, 24 Sturdee Avenue, Rosebank 2196, South Africa

Penguin Books Ltd, Registered Offices: 80 Strand, London WC2R 0RL, England

www.penguin.com

This translation first published 1979

039

Printed and bound in Great Britain by Clays Ltd, Elcograf S.p.A.
Set in Monotype Bembo

www.greenpenguin.co.uk

CONTENTS

❖

GENERAL INTRODUCTION

◆

THE civil law of Rome in its developed form as it has come down to us is undoubtedly one of the greatest achievements of the human mind and spirit. After so many centuries of so-called civilization, progress and culture it is well for twentieth-century man, taking for granted, as he does, that among the plethora of things which the state will provide for him is a system of law which he supposes will ensure justice, and regulate society, to reflect that he owes directly to the Romans the very existence of a theory of such a thing as law. Had that theoretical base not been brought into existence, present-day lifestyles would be unlikely to exist either. The Romans were the first to regard law as a science by means of which they could look at the world, with all its people and property and their intermingling relationships, through juridical concepts every bit as orderly as the concepts used by, say, mathematicians and physicists for their particular observations. European lawyers in particular (the English Channel was largely responsible for a different development in the British Isles – the common law rather than the civil law of Rome) have kept alive many of the basic notions of the ancient Roman law as a basis for their present juridical systems. It was not so much the technical apparatus of the Roman law which proved of such value to them, but its clarity, simplicity and orderliness which have allowed this long and continuous development to take place.

The story is of course a long one – the Emperor Justinian, who brought the ancient law to its finest flowering, died in

8
THE DIGEST OF ROMAN LAW

A.D. 565 – and it is also a complex one, as indeed any history must be of the development of laws which claim to bring system and order to more or less the whole range of human activity, but the enduring nature of the underlying influence of classical Roman law has been graphically – and reasonably – described as being like a duck as it swims, bobs and dives in the water: it hides itself at times, but is never quite lost, always coming up again alive. This idea has been expressed by numerous writers. One of the most fulsome expressions of the continuing (though not necessarily continuous) and pervading (though not all-pervading) influence of Roman law upon subsequent civilization is that of d'Entrèves:[1]

It is no exaggeration to say that, next to the Bible, no book has left a deeper mark upon the history of mankind than the Corpus Iuris Civilis. Much has been written about the impact of Rome upon Western civilization. Much has been disputed about 'the ghost of the Roman Empire' that still lurks far beyond the shores of the Mediterranean. The heritage of Roman law is not a ghost but a living reality. It is present in the court as well as in the market-place. It lives on not only in the institutions but even in the language of all civilized nations.

To the pessimist or the sceptic, who too readily accepts the view that ideologies are nothing but a superstructure of facts, the history of that heritage is a reminder of the predominance of the spiritual over the material factor. 'The history of Roman Law during the Middle Ages testifies to the latent vigour and organizing power of ideas in the midst of shifting surroundings' [Vinogradoff; cf. the 'duck' idea, above]. The revival of Roman Law was a powerful leaven in the transformation of the social and political structure of Europe. Those who speak of a *damnosa hereditas* have their eye only on one side of the picture. They overlook what is our greatest debt to the Roman inheritance: the notion that law is the common patrimony of men, a bond that can overcome their differences and enhance their unity.

1. A. P. d'Entreves, *Natural Law*, p. 17.

Before any evaluation of the place of Roman law in the life of the Roman people and its effects on modern law can be attempted or any verdict passed on the achievement of Justinian, a brief outline will have to be given of the development of the Roman law and the sources from which it was drawn. No system of law can be understood without some knowledge of the history of the society for whose use it was evolved and whose relationships it was intended to regulate. The various standard histories of Rome give detailed accounts of the political and social evolution of the Roman state, of its internal politics and its civil and external wars; many of them also attempt to give some cultural background by reference to Latin literature and Roman building, but it is remarkable that scarcely any of them make more than passing reference to that vital ingredient upon which the much-vaunted Roman administration depended, the Roman law. This is no place to embark upon any sort of general history of Rome, but since even that diminishing number of people who nowadays study ancient history are unlikely to have made acquaintance with Roman legal history, what follows is an attempt to sketch, albeit briefly, the main features of the development of that law so that it may be set into its context against the more familiar history of events in general. Above all it is vital to bear in mind, because of the foreshortening or telescoping effect of looking back upon events far in the past, that the Corpus Iuris Civilis of Justinian, which was completed in A.D. 534, came at the end of a development of laws which had spread over thirteen centuries. English land law is thought to have a long history: indeed it is on this account that it has acquired much of its complexity. Some of its basic notions literally came with the Conqueror; Edward I made far-reaching reforms in statutes which directly affect every conveyance made today, and the extent of legal memory, whereof the mind of man runneth not to the contrary, was set at 1189.

How long ago we think the Conquest was! After all, we recently celebrated .its ninth centenary; and Edward I's statutes will soon be seven hundred years old. Were Justinian embarking upon his *Digest* now he would be thinking back to the mists of time two hundred years before Alfred was burning the cakes in the ancient kingdom of Wessex.

THE SOURCES OF THE LAW

Some understanding of the sources from which the Roman law developed is necessary for an appreciation not only of its growth and its operation, but even of its statement as set out in the *Digest*. The part played by the magistrates and the jurists was critical in the evolution of the law to meet changing circumstances as Rome grew from a small, primarily agricultural city state into the greatest military and trading power of the ancient world and one of the greatest empires in man's history. The perusal of even a short passage of the *Digest*, which is composed almost entirely of revised statements of authority by the jurists, quickly shows also how important was the law of procedure which regulates the forms of action to be employed in particular circumstances in allowing the law to operate with sufficient flexibility, and there are also included quotations from the Edicts, those statements of policy which the magistrates issued upon entry into office as a sort of manifesto indicating their plans for the application of the laws in various situations. The sources, then, of Roman law are traditionally divided into three main streams: statutes, the Edicts of magistrates, and the extensions of principle through the 'interpretation' of the jurists.

(i) *The law-making assemblies*

'*Statute*' means an enactment of a rule of law by the constitutionally appropriate legislative body. In the Roman Republic there were three such bodies: the *comitia centuriata* and the *comitia tributa*, which enacted a form of statute known as *lex* (and often known by the name of its proposer, for example Lex Aquilia, the various Leges Juliae), and the *concilium plebis*. Strictly speaking an enactment of this latter body was *plebiscitum*, and only binding on the plebs and not the whole people unless approved by the Senate. However, this requirement seems to have been abolished by the Lex Hortensia of about 287 B.C. This law was itself a plebiscite (the 'lower house' it seems could impose its will upon the upper, just as our House of Commons seems able to steamroller the House of Lords into accepting measures to restrict its own powers) and *plebiscita* were often referred to as *leges*, especially once they came to bind the whole people.

It is the statute or act of parliament which occurs first to the layman when he thinks of the law. However, in Roman law, just as in our own common law (at least until the recent great increase in state activity in more and more spheres of life, which can only be done by Act, Regulation and Statutory Instrument of Parliament), statutes played a relatively minor part. The English courts and the Roman jurists were a much greater influence, and with their resource and subtlety provided a wealth of detail and flexibility beyond the means of even the most skilled legal draftsman. There was, however, one law of particular and original sanctity to the Romans, which was *lex* and was the foundation stone of the great legal edifice which developed over succeeding centuries – the Law of the Twelve Tables.

The Twelve Tables are the earliest firm statement of any part of Roman law that has come down to us. There are traditions of legislation by the more or less legendary kings, the last of whom, Tarquin the Proud, was expelled from Rome in 510 B.C., but these so-called Laws of the Kings were probably no more than declarations of ancient custom and religious practice. Little is known of them apart from purported citations by non-legal authors and it is quite certain that they played no part in developing the later law. The Twelve Tables are of a wholly different order of importance. Their production was the outcome of one of the phases of the struggles between the 'upper crust' Patricians and the 'common people', the Plebeians. The law had been the preserve of the Patricians and its administration a semi-holy mystery known only to them. The Plebeians, who were the majority of the population, had no knowledge of its content and demanded that it be published. The traditional story is that ten men, the Decemvirs, were sent to Greece in 451 B.C. to study the laws of Solon (at this time, having yet no developed law, the Romans revered the Greeks in this sphere too, though here at least they were later to surpass them), in the light of which they compiled a code which was set up in the market place on ten inscribed bronze tablets. Two more were added a year later and the twelve were approved as a *lex* by the *comitia centuriata* in 450 B.C. They consisted mainly of ancient custom, but there seems also to have been some innovation and some incorporation of what the Decemviri had learned of Greek law. The Gauls are said to have destroyed the original bronzes in the Sacking of Rome in 390 B.C. Be that as it may, the law of the Twelve Tables has not come down to us in its original form, though it is possible to deduce a good deal of it through numerous references in later writings, some of which purport to give quotations. It was, in the course of time and changing conditions, superseded by later laws long before the end of the Republic, but the Twelve Tables continued to be held in great reverence, and Cicero recorded that in his younger days schoolboys had to learn them by heart at school. Such rules as we know are simple, and concerned procedure rather than substantive law, no doubt because the law was already regarded as the proper sphere for experts, whereas a simple idea of procedure was what the common man needed to know. The opening passage gives some idea of the nature of the Twelve Tables:

If a man is summoned to appear in court and does not come, let witnesses be heard and then let the plaintiff seize him. If he resists or absconds, the plaintiff can use force. If he is ill or too old, let the plaintiff provide a beast to bring him: but if he declines this offer, the plaintiff need not provide a carriage ... If a man is killed while committing theft in the night, that killing is lawful.

In the four centuries between the enactment of the Twelve Tables and the end of the Republic we know of only thirty or so statutes affecting public law. The law, however, cannot stand still if the society it serves is changing, and the power of 'interpretation', entrusted at first to the Pontiffs as a quasi-religious mystery, but later to the jurists, coupled with the powers of the magistrates ensured that the law did adapt to the changing requirements of the people.

(ii) *The magistrates*

The superior magistrates of the Republic all possessed the power to issue Edicts, which were probably at first, as has been mentioned, statements of how they intended to fulfil their duties during their year of office. It is from the Edicts of those magistrates who had powers of jurisdiction that there grew up a body of law known as the *ius honorarium* which stood side by side with and in effect modified the operation of the formal rules of the *ius civile* in much the same way as equity developed in England to supplement and temper the much more rigid common law. The most important of the magistrates in this context was the Praetor, for his powers extended over the procedures and remedies of the law, and so even without making any new rules as such he was able indirectly to alter the law by influencing the way in which it was put into practice. His concern was the administration of the private law between citizens, and it was to this end that he had a general supervision over litigation and the granting or withholding of remedies; but in a broader context it was by setting out in his Edict the principles upon which he would act in regulating procedure that he was able to have such a profound effect upon the development of the law.

Modern lawyers tend to look upon the law as conferring rights; primitive lawyers usually look upon the law as a collection of remedies to deal with specific wrongs. This was the case in the old common law of England, which consisted in a number of writs each of which was used to start a particular sort of action for redress of a particular sort of legal wrong. It was also the case at Rome, but the Praetors seem to have realized early on that by granting a new right of action where none existed before, or by extending an existing right to cover new circumstances, they were in practical effect extending or amending the law itself. Eventually the ancient forms of action gave way altogether to a new form, which could be expressed for the court not in the old ritual forms, but in the words of a formula, a statement similar to the pleadings in our modern procedure. Significant though this change was, affecting fundamentally the whole operation of the law and its future development, we do not know exactly when, or how, it took place. It received formal blessing in the Lex Aebutia of uncertain date, though it is generally agreed to have been enacted between 149 and 126 B.C. At any rate the new formulary scheme of procedure was in operation in the last quarter of the second century B.C. Throughout the *Digest* there are references indicative of the Praetor's power through this control over procedure. Discussion of a case frequently ends with a statement that the Praetor will or will not in such circumstances grant an action to the plaintiff.

There were two Praetors in any given year. They held office together, the Urban Praetor being concerned with the people of Rome, who were the prime subjects of the *ius civile*; indeed in its original meaning this term indicated the law which applied to Roman citizens only. The rest of humanity were foreigners (*peregrini*), subject in the eyes of the Romans to the *ius gentium*, the law of everyone else. Such people and such laws were the magisterial concern of the Peregrine Praetor. From the earliest times, citizens must have had disputes with foreigners, so here was a fertile field for the development of new rules of law and adaptation of existing ones. Indeed this flexibility was one of the strengths of Roman law and its adoption of principles based upon the needs and experience of others was one of its sources of growth. The Peregrine Praetor must therefore have been in a very powerful position to make innovations, for he was not working within an existing framework of tradition and practice like the Urban Praetor, and he must have introduced new provisions and procedures much more freely and rapidly than his colleague. However, we have no direct evidence, for although parts of Edicts have come down to us through quotations in the *Digest*, those quotations come from the Urban Praetor's Edict. No fragments of the Peregrine Edict survive, probably because it ceased to be of importance after A.D. 212 when the *Constitutio Antonina* conferred Roman citizenship on all free men living in the Empire.

Provincial governors also had a power to issue Edicts on matters relevant to the governing of their provinces, and Gaius wrote a commentary on this subject, but of all the magistrates who had such powers, only the Aediles have had a significant effect on the development of the law. Their powers extended over the streets and markets and thus it fell to them to supervise trading practices. The slave dealers of Rome would seem to have been the spiritual forebears of bombed-site car dealers of more recent times and a headache to the Aediles, who were concerned to see that honest buyers stood a fair chance at the hands of such people. Through their Edicts they accordingly developed conditions and warranties for quality which were to be implied into contracts of the sale, first of slaves and cattle, and later into all contracts of sale.

(iii) *The Emperor*

Whether or not he realized it at the time, it was in his insistence on a return to Republican constitutional forms that Augustus opened the way for law-making by subsequent Emperors through the *Principum Placita*. The institutional basis upon which this development rested was the power of superior magistrates to issue edicts – hence, if the Emperor be a magistrate, albeit often a perpetual one and albeit very much *primus inter pares*, he could claim to exercise a perfectly normal, wholly traditional, magisterial power. Leaving aside speculation about the extent of his foresight, it seems quite clear that when Augustus became sole ruler and restored to the popular assembly the legislative powers formerly vested in the Triumvirate, this was not intended to restore effective power to the people, but was rather designed as a means of giving him a way of making his will effective. The law by which the people conferred imperial power on him, the Lex de Imperio, gave him absolute discretion in a number of administrative matters, and although the Emperor was at first subject to the laws, he was very soon allowed specific dispensations, though it was not until the third century A.D. that he was openly acknowledged as being above the law. From the beginning, however, despite the emphasis accorded to the continuity of Republican institutions, it is clear that the Emperor was in a special position and that because of it he could exercise a certain legislative power; and from the time of Augustus himself the Emperor had the means, through holding magistracies, of assuming wide-ranging powers over the administration of existing laws (the Praetors' concern) and introducing new ones (the concern of Consuls and Tribunes). Add to this the power to dispense from, suspend, interpret and then to extend *leges*, which began to be accorded to the Emperor almost as soon as Augustus had established his pre-eminence, and it can be seen that here was a formidable power-base from which it became a natural and easy step for the Emperor to assume overall control of law-making, yet always being able to justify himself by reference to the hallowed Republican constitution as and when necessary. Whereas Augustus tended to entrust, say, a Consul with steering through a new law, quite soon, actual legislation by the Emperor was accepted and justified and it was fully recognized by the time of Hadrian that the Emperor could make what were in effect laws; indeed by the third century the Emperor became the sole legislator and Ulpian was able to write: '*Quod principi placuit, legis habet vigorem*' ('What the Emperor pleases has the force of law').

Imperial law-making was eventually effected in a number of ways in addition to the edicts mentioned above. Through the *mandate* he could in effect make law by giving administrative instructions to such officials as provincial governors, which over the years developed into a collection of standing orders. His *decrees*, or judicial decisions made when hearing cases in court, had a special authority simply because they were the considered opinion of the Emperor and thus tended to be regarded with respect by other judges, who would tend to follow them whenever they were relevant to other cases. The famous *rescripts* were written replies to specific points put to the Emperor, who seemed to be available to give his attention to all sorts of inquiries and petitions not only from public officials but also from the humblest private individual. Many of them are preserved in the *Codex* of Justinian, which enables us to see something of their enormous range. Some of them asked for a preliminary ruling on a point of law relevant to a case coming on for hearing, and both judge and litigant could seek guidance in this way; others relate to wholly private and often trivial worries, but all were given on the basis of the 'facts' as stated by the inquirer, so that in the case of pre-litigation inquiries, the Imperial view would not bind the parties if the court found the facts of the case to be other than as claimed. A homely example from the *Codex* (4.44.1) is quoted by Professor Nicholas:[2]

The Emperor Alexander, to Aurelius Maro, soldier. If your father sold the house under duress the transaction will not be upheld, since it was not carried out in good faith; for a purchase in bad faith is void. If therefore you bring an action in your own name the provincial governor will intervene, especially since you declare that you are ready to refund to the buyer the price that was paid.

The names of the consuls for the year were usually added and these too are usually given in the *Codex*. We can thus date this Rescript as being of the year A.D. 222.

(iv) *The Senate*

The Senate is probably, after the Emperor and the army, the Roman institution most widely known to the layman. A few words must therefore be added on the part it played in making law. Under the Republican constitution, though it was greatly respected as an august body of the most important citizens, it had no direct law-making power and its resolu-

2. Barry Nicholas, *An Introduction to Roman Law*, p. 18, note 3.

tions, for all their pomp and deliberation, only took the form of advice to magistrates. Generally, of course, its advice would be followed, but it had the force of law only after embodiment in some enactment made subsequently, either by a *lex* or by an edict of the appropriate magistrate. The Senate's power was thus indirect, and dependent upon the respect accorded to it being sufficient for its views to be enacted into law by others. However, the ancient assemblies which enacted *lex* fell into disuse in the Imperial period and the power of the Senate, apparently simply because it was still there, expanded to fill the resulting constitutional vacuum. Decisions of the Senate (*Senatus consulta*) first seem to have assumed the force of law in the time of the Emperor Hadrian; and Gaius, writing in the second century A.D., said that, though it had been disputed previously, *Senatus consulta* had the force of *lex* in his day. However, by the end of that century the Senate is seen acting simply as a 'rubber stamp', meekly giving its 'authority' to any proposal of the Emperor. He appeared before it, made his proposal in a speech (*oratio*) and it was duly approved. Even if the measure was formally a decision of the Senate it followed so automatically that the subsequent jurists referred to the Emperor's speech itself as the law-making process.

However, through the accidents of history it is the Senate to which the visitor to Rome may nowadays feel closest, especially if physical remains give him any appreciation of events with which they were connected. One may now, nearly two thousand years later, stand in the Curia (the building in which the Senate met) and with a little imagination envisage the procedures and perhaps even picture the debates in that impressive chamber. H. V. Morton has special gifts in this respect and one can, through his eyes, almost see the Senators going about their business of state. This is what he says in *A Traveller in Rome*:[3]

3. H. V. Morton, *A Traveller in Rome*, pp. 98–9.

I had been inspecting the Arch of Septimius Severus, and thinking of the old Emperor swaying through Scotland in his litter, when I noticed a few paces away a flight of steps leading to a battered building entered by two tall bronze doors. I mounted the steps and found that I was standing in the Senate House – the Curia — of ancient Rome, the most famous building in the annals of law and, politically, the most important place in the Roman world.

It was revealed in 1937, when the ancient church of S. Adriano was demolished. As the church came down the Senate House emerged, apparently little the worse for its entombment of thirteen centuries. Beneath the floor was found the original pavement of Diocletian's time, on which the Senate used to meet in those fateful ages before the fall of Rome.

I was astonished by the faces of those around me as they gazed impassively about them, apparently unconscious that the ground on which they stood was historically sacred. Here was indeed the venerable great-grandmother of parliaments. I felt the need to share my delight with someone. I spoke to a man standing beside me, but he replied in some language I could not understand. I remembered Gibbon treading the Forum with a lofty step, and thought how he would have stood in wonder at this sight.

The hall is by no means magnificent and is not large. Three tiers of marble seats face each other along its length and at the end, facing the assembly, the presiding magistrates had their curule chairs. At the far end of the hall there is a mass of brickwork which once held the altar and the famous statue of the golden Victory brought by Augustus from Tarentum.

There were various peculiarities about the Curia. It was a conse-crated building and had the status of a temple. The Senate could not meet before sunrise or after sunset, therefore the all-night sittings of Parliament, so familiar to us, were unknown in ancient Rome. The first act of a Senator when he entered the House was to approach the Altar of Victory and cast a few grains of incense on the brazier which glowed before it. As in our own House of Commons, there was no tribune and speakers addressed the assembly from their seats; when a division was taken, those in favour of the motion moved over to one side and those in opposition to the other.

The building we now see is as it was during the late Empire, at the time of Diocletian. In its long history it has been enlarged, restored, and twice burnt to the ground, but it is believed to occupy the site of the earliest assembly hall of Rome's third king, in 670 B.C., where the elders used to meet in their rough sheepskin coats. In successive buildings on the same site the affairs of the Republic and the Empire were discussed for centuries; from this place the Roman world was ruled; every great man in Roman history had lifted his voice there and its floor has known the tread of every Roman orator and emperor. There was a time in Republican days when the habits of the Senate were so austere and frugal that heating the House in winter was an unthinkable luxury. I remembered a letter written by Cicero to his brother in 62 B.C., in which he said that an important meeting had to be adjourned because of the cold; and members of the public were highly amused by the sight of the revered elders emerging from the icy hall wrapped in their purple-striped togas.

I suppose my interest must have been so marked that the attendant, who guards a barrier to prevent visitors from walking on the old marble, waited until we were alone and then, with a charming and understanding Italian smile, quickly moved the barrier and waved me on to the floor of the Senate. I examined every detail and was interested most of all by the brickwork at the end of the hall, which had held the Altar of Victory that stood in front of the lovely statue from Tarentum. Every theological student will remember the debate in the fourth century about this statue, but who could imagine that its plinth can still be seen?

(v) *The jurists*

No body of law can exist usefully as a mere collection of rules: even the Ten Commandments themselves require interpretation in applying their precepts to the facts of any particular case. Holy Scripture indeed says 'Thou shalt not kill' but in applying even that simple rule we need to be sure what 'kill' may mean precisely, in a given situation and, for example, whether any killing can conceivably ever be justifiable and if so in what circumstances. Thus the Roman *leges* and Edicts, often standing as bald statements, also required 'interpretation' for particular cases. This interpretative function will normally be entrusted to experts who acquire the necessary experience and expertise, and this is usually the function of a lawyer, whose professional skill lies not so much in simply knowing rules as in the ability to analyse the essential facts of his client's case to sort out those which are legally significant, analyse the relevant law and then, through experience and judgement, apply the law as he sees it to the relevant facts as he has deduced them to be. This process was the basis of the lawyer's skill in Rome just as it is today. Leaving aside the earliest days when the law was regarded as a sacred mystery and its administration accordingly entrusted to the Pontiffs – a time which is still shrouded in doubt and about which very little can be said with much certainty – the interpretation of the law was entrusted to the jurists. It was especially the jurists of the so-called classical age who were the real builders of the great fabric of the Roman law. We have already seen that *lex* or statute law provided a relatively small part of the Roman law. The jurists were to Roman law what the common law, derived from the multitude of actual cases before the Courts, is to English law, for they recorded their cases of interest and the points over which they disagreed, and it is this record, in some part no doubt theoretical but mainly derived from practice, which has come down to us in the *Digest*.

Although they had such a great influence upon the development of the Roman law it must be emphasized that they were not professional legal practitioners in the modern sense. Indeed they have no exact parallel in today's world. As the successors to the Pontiffs they were at first men of the leading Patrician families who had studied the law and simply undertook the interpretation of it for others as their contribution to public life. Professor Nicholas points out that they received no remuneration and that the law was only one facet of their public career.[4] Rather than 'lawyers' as we understand the term they were statesmen who were learned in the law; and even though the class from which they tended to come widened in the latter years of the Republic and thereafter, their essential character and cast of mind remained the same. As men of affairs they were interested in practical questions rather than matters of pure theory, but as they were not under the pressures of the daily practice of the law in the courts they could afford the time to speculate as to how the law might apply in certain conditions. They thus filled the roles which nowadays we regard as separate – they were in effect both practical and academic lawyers.

It seems that quite early in the Imperial period Augustus conferred upon certain jurists the right *publice respondendi* – the right or privilege of giving written opinions under seal, authorized by the Emperor and binding on the parties to the case in respect of which the opinion was delivered. Much academic ink has been spilt in considering the precise authority of this right and such questions as whether or not the opinion so delivered was binding upon the judge who heard the case, and this remains one of the unsolved problems of ancient law. We simply do not have the evidence necessary to come to a firm view of these points and indeed even such a basic question as what was the legal effect of conferring the *ius respondendi* is still a mystery. We do not know how many jurists enjoyed this right; indeed we only have direct evidence of the *ius* being conferred upon two jurists – Massurius Sabinus, who received it from Tiberius, and the otherwise unknown Innocentius, upon whom it was conferred by Diocletian. Innocentius certainly lived later than the 'great' age of the jurists, but we do not know how long the practice continued. It may well have been no more than a mark of

4. Barry Nicholas, *An Introduction to Roman Law*, pp. 28–33.

special competence or distinction. If it were, it lost its original significance once all the leading jurists were drawn into the Emperor's service.

Cicero recorded[5] that the jurists were consulted about all sorts of business, not always legal, because of the respect afforded to their opinions, and although this had probably ceased to be true in his own day, he gave a good picture of the part they played in the development of the law. They gave advice to those who came to consult them – and these included not only litigants and citizens with problems, but also the magistrates and the judges. Such consultations might be formal and result in written opinions, but were frequently informal, even a discussion during a walk in the Forum. The jurist also had his part to play when a case actually came to court. Here his business was not to act as advocate – others such as Cicero himself followed that quite separate calling – but rather to act as a sort of consultant to those who were directly concerned in the presentation of the case. Their third function, as listed by Cicero, was to give general assistance in all manner of legal transactions, including, where necessary, the drafting and preparation of legal documents.

All good jurists – and these men were clearly public-spirited and more concerned with esteem than earning a fee anyway – gave instruction in the law, regarding the passing-on of their expertise as a part of their function, just as present-day barristers and solicitors bear the responsibility of giving practical instruction to aspiring barristers who read in Chambers and would-be solicitors who serve their apprenticeship as articled clerks. Similarly, the young Roman 'sat in' with his master as he did his daily work and thus acquired his practical 'know-how' from cases as they arose, rather than as an abstract

5. Cicero, *De Oratore* 3.33.133–135; see also 1.48.212; *Pro Murena* 9.19; *Topica* 5.28; and see Justinian, *Digest* 1.2.2.37.

theory. This apprenticeship system with its tradition of directly instructing pupils by personal advice and example gave rise by the time of Hadrian to two 'schools' or sects of jurists which are said by Pomponius to have been founded by Labeo and Capito and may have developed their traditional differences from the personal and political rivalry alleged to have existed between Autistius Labeo, who was described by Buckland as 'the republican, a man of independent mind and prone to innovation', and Ateius Capito, 'the adherent of the empire, inclined to follow tradition and to rest upon authority'.[6] Their 'schools' probably developed gradually and are generally known by the names of later leaders, the school of Labeo being called the Proculians (after Proculus) and the school of Capito being called the Sabinians, after Sabinus. Julian, a Sabinian, is the last jurist known to have been a member of a particular school; Gaius says that he himself was a Sabinian, but they probably had little if any organized existence by his time and certainly died out before the end of the second century. One cannot proceed far into the literature of the Roman law without being made aware of the existence of these 'schools' and many of the differences between them, but despite the best efforts of numerous learned authorities it is not possible to discern any consistency in the divergences between them which could fairly be said to indicate any coherent philosophy or approach on either side. The following typical example gives an idea of how points were made and discussed. Gaius says:

If you make wine, oil or grain out of my grapes, olives or ears of corn, the question arises whether that wine, oil or grain is mine or yours. Again, if you make a utensil from my gold or silver, or fashion a boat, chest or chair with my planks of wood, or make a garment from my wool, mead from my wine and honey, or a plaster or eye-

6. W. W. Buckland, *A Textbook of Roman Law*, p. 26.

salve from my drugs, the question arises whether what you have made in this way out of my property is yours or mine. Some people think it is the basic material that counts, that is to say that the manufactured article should be held to belong to the owner of the materials from which it was made, and this is the view preferred by Sabinus and Cassius: but others think it belongs to its maker and this is the opinion of the authorities of the other school. They add, however, that the former owner of the materials has an action in theft against the person who took them as well as an action to recover their value, because although things which have ceased to exist cannot be recovered in kind, they may still be the subject of an action for their value against thieves and certain other possessors. (Gaius, *Institutes* II.79)

Justinian settles the disputed point thus:

After many arguments between the Proculians and Sabinians it seemed best to adopt the middle view of those who thought that if the thing made can be reduced again to its original material, he who was owner of that material owns the thing: but if it cannot be so reduced, he who made it is the owner of it. For example, a cast vase can easily be melted down to a lump of brass, silver or gold; but wine, oil or flour cannot be turned back into grapes, olives or ears of corn, nor can mead be reduced into wine and honey. However, if someone makes a new thing partly from his own materials and partly from someone else's, for example mead with his own wine and someone else's honey, or a plaster or eyesalve partly with his own and partly with another's drugs or a garment from wool partly his and partly someone else's, in all such cases he who made the thing is certainly the owner of it, for he not only did the work, but also provided part of the materials. (*Institutes* 2.1.25)

There were of course provisions to deal with the matter of compensation once the question of ownership had been decided.

Vital though the jurists' teaching function was in the legal life of Rome, for us their writing was even more important as it is through this medium that their work has been preserved, even though indirectly. We know that the literature produced by the jurists was enormous, but most of it has disappeared, and has come to us only through the quotations preserved in the *Digest*. There are indeed fragments of originals, some large and some very small, but the only work to have survived in anything approaching entirety is the *Institutes* of Gaius. This was an elementary textbook for students, as was the *Regulae* of Ulpian (of which a good deal also survives). The jurists are known to have produced in addition more advanced treatises for instructional purposes; collections of opinions for practitioners; systematic expositions of the civil law and works akin to present-day monographs on particular aspects of the law or even on earlier writers – Pomponius, Paul and Ulpian all wrote their own commentaries on Sabinus's textbook on the civil law. It is thought that Paul probably produced more 'books' than any other of the jurists – at least, more works by him can be deduced to have existed through the quotations and references made in the *Digest*. The list is impressive – eighty major works in 275 'books' (a book running to between thirty and fifty pages of this volume).

Thirty-nine writers are quoted in the *Digest*, but of these Gaius, Julian, Papinian, Paul and Ulpian appear much more frequently than any others, and their works make up by far the greater part of it. The reason why their works exist for us only at second hand is that Justinian, intending his *Digest* to be of unquestionable authority, forbade any future direct citation of the original works upon which it was based (and also the making of any commentary upon his *Digest*) so that they tended to die of neglect. Purely by chance, however, in 1816 Niebuhr,[7] who was working in the Cathedral library at

7. Barthold Georg Niebuhr (1776–1831) was Prussian Ambassador to the Holy See 1816–23, and Professor of Roman History at Bonn 1823–31. His *History of Rome* was written between 1811 and 1832.

Verona on an early text of St Jerome, found underneath it a juristic writing which proved to be the *Institutes* of Gaius. This book had long been thought to have been the model for Justinian's own *Institutes*, but only after Niebuhr's discovery could this be positively confirmed. This text dates from the fifth or sixth century, and the belief that it contained Gaius's text substantially as he left it was confirmed by comparison with some pages of a fourth or fifth century manuscript found in Egypt in 1933, which coincided.

The existence of this work in some ways brings Gaius much closer to us than those other jurists of whom we know only through quotation. Buckland however refers to him as the most mysterious person who plays a large part in the Roman law, for although we have a complete work by him we know relatively little of him as a man. He was born in the reign of Hadrian and was a teacher of the law, though he may never have had the *ius respondendi* conferred upon him. It is probable that he was not deemed eminent in his own day, for no other classical jurist seems to have quoted him or relied upon him as an authority, but his reputation grew after his death and he came to be regarded with the peculiar affection implicit in references to him as 'Gaius noster' (our Gaius) – even though only his praenomen is known and it is not possible to give dates for his birth and death with any confidence. All that can be said with certainty is that he flourished in the first half of the second century A.D., so he was probably born between A.D. 70 and 80. Mommsen[8] thought he was a Greek provincial; others would have it that he came from Troas, that he taught in Beirut, but he remains a shadowy figure, albeit one regarded with greater affection than any other jurist.

Julian (Salvius Julianus) was not only relied upon to a much greater extent for the *Digest*, but was a much more distinct

8. Theodor Mommsen (1817–1903) was Professor of Ancient History at Berlin 1858–1903. His *Roman History* was published in 1854–6.

figure. He held many of the great offices of state under Hadrian and Antoninus Pius, was paid twice the usual fees on account of his great and revered learning, and was the friend and confidant of Emperors. He died in the reign of Marcus Aurelius, who described him in a rescript as '*amicus noster*'. He was the last recorded leader of the Sabinian school, but it is generally thought that he had too powerful and wide-ranging an intellect to be tied down to the viewpoints of any particular sect. We hear of no more Proculians after his time and this may well be because of the predominance which the Sabinians established through Julian's weighty authority. His writings were probably the model upon which Justinian's *Digest* was based – in which case we may ascribe to him the greatest influence of any of the jurists on the overall develop-ment of the civil law in later centuries. Buckland says that the principal characteristics of Julian's work seem to be a very lucid style and a clear recognition of the fact that legal con-ceptions must move with the times, and he accorded him the extraordinary compliment that he played a part in Roman law akin to that of Lord Mansfield in the development of the com-mon law of England, elucidating principles and sweeping away unreal and pedantic distinctions.

Papinian (Aemilius Papinianus) has a particular connection with England, having accompanied the Emperor Septimius Severus to York as Prefect in 208. He was born between 148 and 153 and was appointed by Severus to be Prefect of the Praetorian Guard, but he was murdered in 212 on the orders of the Emperor Caracalla when he refused to make a public declaration approving of Caracalla's murder of his brother Gaeta. The Romans themselves regarded Papinian as the greatest of the jurists, though modern commentators would mostly rate Julian higher, while some of them would also place Ulpian higher than Papinian. Those nearer to him how-ever may have been better able to assess him, for his reputation probably rested mainly upon his practical work. Unfortunately he wrote no comprehensive treatise and Buckland's view is that his chief works, *Quaestiones* and *Responsa*, which cover much ground, show a judicial and critical mind rather than great intellectual fertility.

Paul (Julius Paulus) was a younger contemporary of Papinian, having been Assessor to him during his Prefectship of the Praetorian Guard. He was a man of affairs in Rome who held high political office and became a member of the imperial council and a fluent and copious legal writer. One of his works, *Sententiae*, has chanced to survive in its original form, but we have a great deal more via quotation in the *Digest*, of which his extracts make up about one-sixth of the whole. There are indeed as many citations from Paul as there are from Ulpian, but the passages from Ulpian tend to be a good deal longer. Modern opinions have differed surprisingly widely over where he should stand in the juristic 'hierarchy': some describe him as profound and original, while others think he was a mere popularizer of no serious significance as a contributor to the development of the law. Maybe like most people it is simply that not everything he did was outstanding – at all events, we have to rely on him a great deal through the accidents of what has come down to us, and from that we can see that at times he makes astute observations and clearly relishes a 'nice' distinction.

Ulpian (Domitius Ulpianus) was also a man of affairs and a participant in Roman politics. He too served in the Emperor's council, under both Severus, to whom he was related, and Caracalla. He became Prefect of the Praetorian Guard and was murdered by his own men. Quotations from Ulpian's works account for about one-third of the *Digest*; Ulpian and Paul together make up half. Buckland's view is that this did not happen because Ulpian was the greatest of the jurists, but more probably simply happened because he was the latest of them. When the *Digest* was being compiled, Ulpian's works were the most recent by a systematic writer of authority and, as Buckland points out, other things being equal, the more up to date a law book is, the better it is. Ulpian had the advantage of the works of the writers who had gone before: in his own day the great age of development in jurisprudence was ending – if it had not already ended – and it fell to him to set forth the result of it all, without the need, perhaps, for great gifts on his own part. This view leads to the conclusion that he was not so much gifted as happening to be in the right place at the right time. However, it is only fair to add (as Buckland very fairly did) that this is only the modern view: in the Middle Ages Ulpian was especially respected and his name was a virtual synonym for Roman law. One book of Ulpian's has survived more or less intact, a fourth-century manuscript of his *Regulae*.

With the murder of Ulpian in 223[9] the line of jurists comes to an abrupt end. Marcian (a younger contemporary of Paul and Ulpian) and Modestinus (a pupil of Ulpian and Prefect of the Praetorian Guard *c.* 226–244) are indeed later, and Modestinus was one of the 'Favoured Five' of the Law of Citations, but even if we add in the only two others of a century later who appear in the *Digest* – Arcadius and Hermogenianus – it is safe to say that no jurist after Ulpian played a part of any significance in the development of the Roman law. Several causes have been advanced as explanations for the sudden termination of an endeavour which for so long had attracted many of the best minds in the Roman world. No single one is likely to provide the whole answer – indeed the demise of the jurists, and with them their science of juris-

9. The date of Ulpian's murder has traditionally been given as 228 and this is stated in most of the legal and historical textbooks. Recently, however, Modrzejewski has advanced convincing arguments for his murder having occurred in 223 (see *R.H.D.*, 1967, pp. 565 ff.).

prudence, must have happened through a coincidence of several factors. As to whether or not these factors coincided by historical accident opinions differ. First, it could not have escaped notice that both Papinian and Ulpian were murdered, and while there are no grounds to suppose the jurists were not reasonably courageous men, simply to be a jurist is not like having a faith to inspire a man, if necessary, even to death. Secondly, the Pax Romana was beginning to break down and with it much of the very fabric of society as it had been known beyond the extent of man's memory. Law of course evolves by adaptation to change, so change itself is far from destructive of legal development; but a change from peaceful conditions to turmoil does seem to be destructive of the development of jurisprudence. Throughout recorded history it would seem that a period of peace, or at least relative calm, is a necessary prerequisite to the flowering of legal talent. In order to produce good law it would seem that good, orderly conditions are vital. There is no point in devoting the labours of the best minds to the law in times when the law counts for little and brute force for much. The best intellects at this time seem to have turned away from the law, which becomes a barren and even futile pursuit in such conditions, and devoted themselves to the newer and more appropriate study – Christianity: this world was less and less attractive to the thinking man, and the thinking man interested in law found even more disagreeable the growing absolutism of the Emperor. In such circumstances one can imagine the greater attractions of a religious philosophy concerned not only with this world but which had a particular message for the next. This is not to say that study of theology was of itself destructive of jurisprudence, only that at that time it seems to have been a more attractive proposition upon which the leading intellects of the day preferred to expend their efforts.

The decay of legal science is evidenced by several enactments showing greater emphasis being placed upon the works of earlier jurists to compensate for the poverty or lack of more recent authorities, a process which reached its nadir in the Law of Citations in 426. The Emperor now made law and no one else, yet the mass of existing authorities had to be placed in some sort of order – here we find what had once been the end of careful legal analysis and considered judgement become simply a process of counting heads. The law said that the writings of Papinian, Paul, Ulpian, Gaius and Modestinus were confirmed as being authoritative and could therefore be cited, except for the notes of Paul and Ulpian on Papinian. Strangely, it was added that Gaius was to have the same authority as the other named jurists. Even more strangely Julian was omitted. Furthermore, other writers cited and approved by the chosen five were also to be deemed as authoritative, provided the citations to be relied upon could be confirmed by comparison of manuscripts (a precaution no doubt necessary because of the antiquity of, for example, Sabinus or Scaevola and the unreliability of copyists). If the authorities cited did not all agree upon the point in question, the majority view was to be followed; if the numbers were equal, the side favoured by Papinian was to prevail, but if he was silent, the judge could make up his own mind. The Law of Citations has been roundly castigated by almost all the modern authorities, mainly on the grounds that legal opinions should be judged by their weight rather than their number and also that there is no logic in the preponderance accorded to Papinian. Theodosius and Valentinian, however, the makers of the law, no doubt had a practical problem to solve and no better means available. They saw the value of a revision of the great and by then unmanageable mass of juristic writings and even proposed that a codification should be made, but this proved impossible because of the lack of men with the necessary talent. A century later Justinian, who found the same problems still remaining, was at least able to profit from the flowering in his day of the law school at Beirut. Long before his time, however, others had seen the value of codifying the juristic materials and made attempts to set out such principles as could be deduced in an orderly and systematic manner. But, though they made their attempts, they all seemed to lack the skilled men needed to make a success of such a project.

The earliest attempt to make a code was the collation of imperial enactments known as the *Codex Gregorianus*, which was published about 300. None of it has been preserved, nor has the bulky *Codex Hermogenianus* of about 365 survived, and we know of them only through quotations in inferior late literature and the so-called barbarian codes. Perhaps the most famous of these 'barbarian' codes was the Lex Romana Visigothorum or *Breviary* of Alaric II published by him in 506. The men who produced it intended to remove the errors and obscurities which had accumulated in the Roman law over so many centuries, but it seems that they lacked the necessary subtlety and sensitivity as well as the legal education to achieve what they hoped, and dealt only with what they thought they understood. It thus had few merits as a work of legal science, but it has enabled us to get a good idea of the text of the *Code* of Theodosius, which was a significant work, produced by a commission of lawyers appointed in 429 and published in 438. Theodosius undoubtedly appreciated the sorry state into which the study of Roman law had declined and having tried to establish some sort of order, however crudely, by the Law of Citations he refounded the law school at Constantinople. His *Code* however has not survived and is known to us only through being cited at length in the *Breviary* of Alaric. The *Code* of the Visigoths was followed soon by the *Code* of Theodoric for the Eastern Goths, and the

Lex Romana Burgundionum also dates from about the same time. None of these works has survived other than at second hand, but the knowledge we do have of them leads to the conclusion that they were no better, if no worse, than one would expect as products of an era generally inimical to the study and development of law. They were probably little more than straightforward attempts to establish some sort of clarity at least of elementary principle at a time of ever-increasing chaos and uncertainty.

It is no small part of the measure of Justinian's greatness that he had the vision to see the value of the law in the order of things that he sought to create and realized the sad state of decline in which the law was languishing, compared with its former glory and elegance. Maybe he consciously connected the time of Rome's peacefulness and pre-eminence with the general respect there then was for the law and its administration, and in seeking to restore that happy state of the past he concluded that the restoration of the law to its former position of esteem and authority must be a part of his programme. The first cracks in the solidity of the Empire had appeared in, say, 251 when the Emperor Decius was killed by the Goths, or 260 when his successor was captured and carted off to die in captivity in Persia, and although the situation was largely restored by Diocletian and Constantine, serious general decline set in about 400 when the last of the legions left Britain for the last time, and it was well under way when Rome itself was sacked by the Goths in 410. By 500 all the western half of the Empire had been lost to the barbarian hordes, Vandals, Goths, Franks, Burgundians, Angles and Saxons. Looking back to the peace of the Empire as established by Augustus and lasting well into the third century, Justinian may well have agreed with Gibbon's verdict:[10]

10. Edward Gibbon, *Decline and Fall of the Roman Empire*, Ch. 3.

If a man were called to fix the period in the history of the world during which the condition of the human race was most happy and prosperous he would without hesitation name that which elapsed from the death of Domitian to the accession of Commodus (A.D. 96–180).

When Justinian became Emperor in 527 in succession to his old uncle Justin, he must already have contemplated for some time his self-appointed two-fold task of restoring the lost provinces to the Empire and providing them with the sort of firm, law-based government which they needed and had formerly enjoyed in the days of Rome's glory, so quickly did he take action on both fronts. The first part of the plan was achieved through great victories in bloody wars which were brilliantly conducted by his great general, Belisarius. The second was placed under the direction of a man of equally outstanding abilities, 'the eminent Tribonian', though he has received less popular fame than the great soldier, no doubt because the work of the law reformer is of necessity less likely to catch the public eye and general imagination: to raise a siege of Rome is more glamorous than carefully to amend a juristic text, though in terms of lasting benefit to the state and good government of the people the latter may well prove to be a greater good for a greater number.

That Justinian felt he had a divine commission for both tasks is evident from his dedications of his legal works, which several times over refer to the gifts given him by God both to vanquish his foes and to establish his laws – indeed his own explanation of the plan of the Digest itself is given in an Imperial Constitution *Deo Auctore* (By God's Authority):

We govern under the authority of God our empire which was delivered to us by His Divine Majesty, we prosecute wars with success, we adorn peace, we hold up the framework of the State and we so lift up our mind in contemplating the aid of the Omnipotent

God, that we do not put our faith in our arms nor in our soldiers, nor in our leaders in war nor even in our own skill, but we rest all our hopes in the providence of the Supreme Trinity and in Him alone, whence have proceeded the elements of the whole universe and by whom their disposition throughout the earth's globe was planned.

Before considering the process by which Justinian's codification of the vast mass of the law was achieved it is well to consider not only the enormity of the task confronting the Commission appointed to undertake it but also the physical size of their resulting work. The whole body of the Corpus Iuris Civilis (which contains not only the *Digest*, but all of Justinian's codified laws) as published by them after revision of the sources and rearrangement in an orderly code covers over 2,200 closely packed quarto pages in the three volumes of the now standard 'Berlin' edition of Mommsen, Krueger, Schoell and Kroll which was published in the last quarter of the nineteenth century. That was, however, only the end product: another way of looking at the epic scale of the undertaking was that of Justinian himself – he points out that the Commission preparing the *Digest* alone read and examined something like 2,000 'books', amounting to 3,000,000 lines. By that method of calculation the Digest can be said to amount to a mere 150,000 lines – and it is about one and a half times the size of the Bible.

THE MAKING OF JUSTINIAN'S CODE

As the Emperor and the issuer of the authoritative commission for the work, Justinian is the man whose name 'appears on the cover' and who has since been given most, if not all, the credit for the great undertaking. However, he was not himself a trained lawyer, and there is no doubt that he relied very heavily upon Tribonian for the organizing and doing of the work. He certainly appears very prominently in all parts of the *Code*, not least in Justinian's introductory paragraphs where even the Emperor himself acknowledges the part played by the 'eminent Tribonian'. The more interesting speculation is as to whether he might have been the inspirer of the whole enterprise as well as the leading contributor to it. Some weight is given to that speculation by the fact that when Tribonian died, the work came abruptly to a halt and Justinian's legislative activity virtually ceased. Be that as it may, let us now turn to the actual work of construction of Justinian's *Code*.

The first Code

Taking his cue from Theodosius II, Justinian first attempted the relatively modest task of updating the code of Imperial Enactments. The *Code* of Theodosius was ninety years old, and there was a need to consolidate that and other codes, omitting what was out of date or overruled, making corrections as necessary, and restating the whole in up-to-date and, if possible, simple language. The Commission of Ten, headed by Tribonian who was then chief of the imperial chancery, was appointed by Justinian in 528 and, incredibly, the new *Code* was promulgated in April 529. Its life was short, however, for it was soon superseded.

The Digest

This was Justinian's biggest and best-known work, being a codification of the enormous mass of juristic writings. It was begun in 530 and published in 533 – another scarcely credible example of fast working by the Commission, which this time consisted of sixteen experts, headed by Tribonian and appointed by him under the Emperor's authority. It was originally expected that the Commission would need ten years to produce the *Digest* when Tribonian received his commission on 15 December 530. Of his sixteen chosen experts, one was, in modern terms, a civil servant, eleven were legal practitioners, and four were professors of law, two from Constantinople and two from Beirut. Their charge was to examine the existing juristic writings and collect together excerpts arranged into fifty books subdivided according to subject matter; to ensure that the law was clearly stated without repetition or contradiction; to remove all obsolete matter and include only up-to-date law; and to give the attribution of each passage. They were free to give what they regarded as the best view in cases of conflict and were not bound by head-counting, as in the Law of Citations, and the notes of Paul, Ulpian and Marcellus, which had been excluded by that law, were not be to neglected on that account. Abbreviations were not to be used, to ensure accuracy; the work was to be the sole authority for the laws and juristic writings to which it referred and no objection could be made even in cases of differences from the originals, which were superseded by it. Finally, no commentaries were to be made.

The fifty books of the *Digest* contain material from the writings of thirty-nine jurists, the earliest of whom was Quintus Mucius Scaevola, who died in 82 B.C. The only others from the Republican era who appear by way of extract are Alfenus and Aelius Gallus, and the great bulk of the finished work is drawn from authors writing between A.D. 100 and 250. There are 2,464 extracts from Ulpian, 2,081 from Paul, 601 from Papinian, 578 from Pomponius, 535 from Gaius; all the rest account for 2,883. Of these five named, Pomponius was the earliest and died in 138, while the latest, Ulpian, was murdered in 223.

Even a brief acquaintance with the *Digest* shows the reader that the Commission did not remove all contradictions or ensure that no repetitions were included. Indeed, the work of cross-checking seems to have been one of the main casualties of the speed of working. It is beyond doubt that all sixteen experts did not read all 2,000 existing books and that they must have worked in committees. It seems that there were three committees for the preparatory work and that for reasons of practicality the labour must have been further subdivided. The final ordering of the excerpts on each subject was puzzling for centuries. The same topic is often discussed at quite separate points in a title with no obvious reason for the separation, and at times there seems to be no reasoned order at all, but the work of Bluhme[11] published in 1818 explained these problems quite convincingly by advancing a theory of how the work was done. He envisaged three committees approaching the various topics and specializing for obvious reasons. One committee took the works of Ulpian on Sabinus and writings dealing with the same topics: Bluhme called this the Sabinian mass. The second committee dealt with the writings of Ulpian on the Praetorian Edict and the civil law matters incorporated into the Edict by Julian (the Edictal mass), while the third took the writings of Papinian and others dealing with the same subjects (the Papinian mass). Sometimes at the end of a title there are references to other books which do not fit any of the above groups or masses and are referred to as the post-Papinian mass or Appendix. It may simply be that, as the Papinian mass was the smallest of the three, that committee was asked to deal with the remaining writings because they may well have completed their examination first. Bluhme envisaged the committees working separately and then meeting to collate their approved extracts and incorporate them into the previously agreed

11. F. Bluhme, *Zeitschrift für Geschichtliche Rechtswissenschaft*, IV, 257 ff.

arrangement of titles. The most important statements were usually placed first, followed by other extracts as they thought fit. The most common arrangement was as above, the Sabinian mass providing the first statement, followed by the Edictal, then the Papinian and finally the Appendix, giving the order often expressed as SEPA. However, every possible order is found.

It will be noticed that at the time of the compilation of the *Digest* most of the material from which it was derived was over three hundred years old, and yet the law was to be stated in a form correct for the time of publication. Furthermore, although Justinian proclaimed his Christianity at the outset of all the works published under his authority, the great bulk of the law was drawn from jurists who flourished before Christianity became the official religion of the Empire. The compilers were accordingly given authority to alter the statements of the jurists where necessary, so that the law was stated in the *Digest* as current for 533. This has become a crucial factor in the study of the development of Roman law, bearing in mind that it was to be the sole authoritative statement of the law, superseding all that had gone before. The previous authorities have virtually all been destroyed or lost and the *Digest* is thus not only our record of Justinian's law but our sole record of the earlier law as well; we cannot necessarily rely upon a statement of, say, Ulpian in the *Digest* as being a correct statement of the law in his time. It would already have been old when the compilers considered it, and even if they made no change, it may well have attracted glosses or corruptions in the intervening three hundred years. There are thus both accidental and intentional changes to be borne in mind when seeking to discover even what the law was in the time of the jurist purporting to make a statement attributed to him. It is an even more engaging pastime to try to deduce, as Professor Alan Watson has recently done, what

the law was in the later years of the Republic.[12] A great deal
of reading between the lines is necessary to engage in dis-
covering these 'interpolations' as they are called, and indeed
interpolation-hunting has long been a favourite sport amongst
Roman lawyers.

No more than a brief indication of the nature, scope and
creation of one of the great works of human endeavour can
be attempted here. Scholars have produced many learned
works about the *Digest*, Justinian's legislation and Roman law
and history which enable the interested reader to pursue
further any aspects about which he wishes to know more. A
short bibliography is therefore included on pp. 190–91.

Before we turn to some passages from the *Digest* itself, brief
mention must also be made of the other parts of Justinian's
scheme. It was clear from the earliest stages of the work on
the *Digest* that it would be an enormous body of material.
The Roman lawyers of the sixth century were, however, just
as mindful of the need to educate their successors as their
predecessors had been and, indeed, members of the legal
profession are just as concerned today. Justinian therefore
asked Tribonian and two of his professional colleagues,
Theophilus from Constantinople and Dorotheus from Beirut,
to prepare an elementary textbook for students from which
they could learn the principles of the law and through which
they would be guided to the *Digest* itself. Taking the *Institutes* of Gaius as their model, they produced the *Institutes* of
Justinian which was also published in December 533 and
given the force of law – which soon proved inconvenient,
for again the cross-referencing was not very efficient and at
times rules are stated differently in *Digest* and *Institutes*. The

12. W. A. J. Watson, *Law of Obligations in the Later Roman Republic*;
Law of Persons in the Later Roman Republic; *Law of Property in the Later
Roman Republic*; *Law-making in the Later Roman Republic*.

main rules of law are stated dogmatically, few reasons are given, though those that are may seem insufferably priggish or engagingly naïve according to the reader's mood of the moment; for example:

(a) In discussing whether one partner may sue another by the special partnership action, the question is raised whether the action lies only for malicious harm or for mere carelessness. Justinian says there is no liability on a partner who has been as careful of partnership assets as he is of his own property 'for he who takes as a partner a person of careless habits has only himself to blame' and must set down any loss to his own lack of care in choosing such a partner (*Institutes* 3.25.8). (Reasons are given much more frequently as part of the fuller treatment and discussion of topics in the *Digest*. There, too, having only oneself to blame is a favourite remark, witness the mule-driver in *Digest* 9.2.8, and the man having a haircut who gets his throat cut instead in *Digest* 9.2.11 (see pp. 75, 76 below).)

(b) 'Fowls and geese are not naturally wild, which we may deduce from the fact that there are particular species which we call "wild fowl" and "wild geese"' (*Institutes* 2.1.16).

(c) 'What non-manifest theft is may be gathered from what we have said, for theft which is not manifest is non-manifest theft' (*Institutes* 4.1.3).

Generally, however, Justinian's *Institutes* have much less colour and character than those of Gaius, a feature which may well be accounted for in their largely derivative nature. The introduction to the *Institutes*, however, is a splendid passage, and not only sheds light on the object of producing the book, but also gives some insight into the preparation of the *Code* and the *Digest*.

IN THE NAME OF OUR LORD
JESUS CHRIST

THE EMPEROR CAESAR FLAVIUS JUSTINIANUS, CONQUEROR OF THE ALAMANNI, GOTHS, FRANKS, GERMANS, ANTES, ALANI, VANDALS, AND AFRICANS, PIOUS, HAPPY, AND GLORIOUS, CONQUEROR AND VANQUISHER, TO YOUNG MEN DESIROUS OF LEARNING THE LAW, GREETING.

Imperial majesty should not only be adorned with military might but also graced by laws, so that in times of peace and war alike the state may be governed aright and so that the Emperor of Rome may not only shine forth victorious on the battlefield, but may also by every legal means cast out the wickednesses of the perverters of justice, and thus at one and the same time prove as assiduous in upholding the law as he is triumphant over his vanquished foes.

This double objective we have achieved with the blessing of God through our utmost watchfulness and foresight. The barbarian races brought under our yoke know well our military achievements; and Africa also and countless other provinces bear witness to our power having been after so long an interval restored to the dominion of Rome and to our Empire by our victories which we have gained through the inspiration of Divine guidance. Moreover, all these peoples are now also governed by laws which we ourselves have promulgated or compiled.

When we had elucidated and brought into perfect harmony the revered imperial constitutions which were previously in confusion, we turned our attention to the immense mass of ancient jurisprudence. Now, by the grace of Heaven, we have completed this work of which even we at one time despaired like sailors crossing the open ocean.

After that task had been accomplished with God's blessing, we summoned together the most excellent Tribonian, Master and former Treasurer of our sacred Palace, and the illustrious professors of law

Theophilus and Dorotheus, who have all on numerous occasions proved to us their ability and legal skill as well as their obedience to our orders; and we specially charged them to compose these our *Institutes* under our authority and guidance, so that you will no longer have to learn the first principles of the law from old and erroneous sources, but can now understand them in the brilliant light of our imperial wisdom. We have also ensured that your ears and minds shall receive only what obtains in current practice and nothing that is unnecessary or erroneous. Accordingly, whereas hitherto law students could scarcely comprehend the imperial constitutions even after three years' study, you, who have been deemed worthy of such a great honour and blessing as to receive both your first lessons and the completion of your legal studies from the very mouth of the Emperor himself, may now even begin your studies by reading them.

Therefore, when we had compiled the Fifty Books called the *Digest* or *Pandects* in which all the ancient law was gathered, with the assistance of the eminent Tribonian aforementioned and of other distinguished and learned men, we directed that these our *Institutes* should be divided into four books containing the first elements of the whole science of law. In these books the law previously in force is briefly stated as well as that which had fallen into disuse but has now been brought to light by the imperial authority. These our *Institutes* thus compiled from all the institutes left by the ancient authorities – especially from the commentaries of our Gaius, particularly his *Institutes* and his work *On Daily Business*, but from many other commentaries also – were brought to us by the three learned men we have referred to above. We have read them and understood them and have accorded them the full force of law.

Therefore receive with eagerness these our laws and study them with cheerful diligence, and prove yourselves persons of such learning that you may entertain the wondrous hope that on completion of your legal studies you may even be able to help govern our Empire in the station allotted to you.

Given at Constantinople 21 November 533 in the third consulate of the Emperor Justinian, ever August.

Though the *Code*, *Digest* and *Institutes* form the great bulk of Justinian's codification of the law and the *Digest* and *Institutes* have had the most lasting value, they do not represent the whole of his work in this field. While the work was being done, the state still had to run and daily life went on, and legislation continued to be passed, some of it of course being intended to settle old disputes, some making new law. A collection of such legislation was made in 530 and published as the *50 Decisions* (*Quinquaginta Decisiones*). It has not survived, but it made the first code obsolete, so Tribonian was commissioned to produce a second code of Imperial Enactments. This was published on 16 November 534 as the *Codex Repetitae Praelectionis* and came into force on 29 December of that year. This code has survived. It is about half the size of the *Digest* and contains about 5,000 enactments, the earliest of which were made by Hadrian. There are twelve books, arranged in titles and dealing with Church Law, Sources, Functions of Officials, Private Law, Criminal Law and Administrative Law. The *Digest* and this second code were intended to be read together as one body of law, but again, the cross-referencing was not good and one cannot always tell that a matter omitted in one is not dealt with in the other, or that a matter which is dealt with in one place is not dealt with differently elsewhere.

Justinian's codification was then complete; but the law obstinately refused to stand still, and the Emperor and his experts had to turn their attention to dealing with the continuing stream of new enactments. Being 'new', in the sense of being made since the *Code*, they were referred to as the *Novellae Constitutiones*, from which they take their modern name of the 'Novels'. They were intended to be officially collected and published from time to time, but they never were. We know of a few through private and unofficial collections, but in any case the flow seems suddenly to have stopped on the death of Tribonian in 546. An epitome of about 120 Novels dated up to 555 was published in Greek in Justinian's own time, but they cannot be said to be a significant addition to the monumental works which were not only the greatest achievement of Justinian's reign, but proved to be one of the most significant influences upon human society ever since.

THE LEGAL BACKGROUND

◈

A DEGREE of technicality is inevitable in the exposition of laws and very often specialist knowledge is also necessary to understand them. Mastery of the technicalities, explanation to laymen, representation of parties in dispute and the training of the next generation are, and always have been, the stock-in-trade of the professional lawyer. The affairs of men make the lawyer a necessary member of our society today, just as he was a part of Roman society: indeed his skills and services seem to be required in every developed type of society. This being so, the reader who enters into the lawyer's special sphere will often find himself in strange territory – the more so when the subject of his reading is not the law of his own day, but the law of a different civilization from a different period of history. The General Introduction has given some idea of the background of the Roman lawyers and the production of the *Digest*. These notes are intended to provide an explanation of a number of technical terms, which cannot be rendered into English simply by the processes of translation, but which need to be understood either because they relate to some part of the Roman legal procedure or because they refer to some institution of the law which is a necessary element in a case or situation being discussed by the juristic writer. No more than the briefest outline to enable the lay reader to understand the jurist's point can be given here. The indulgence of the lawyer is sought in respect of the inevitable 'loose ends'. The law became an almost complete web and taking out any single topic cannot but leave unfinished some strands which lead directly from it into other subjects.

The Roman institutional writers divided their accounts of the law into sections relating to Persons, Things (property and obligations) and Actions (legal procedure). This is the pattern adopted by Gaius in his *Institutes* and followed in the *Institutes* of Justinian.

PERSONS

(i) *Freemen and slaves*

The 'standard unit' of the Roman law was the freeborn Roman citizen, male, of age and sound mind and head of his family. Everyone else was legally inferior and by comparison subject to some sort of restriction, ranging from minor to total, upon his legal powers, rights or personality. There thus developed a stratified society in which every man had his legally appointed and legally defined place.

Gaius says: 'The main distinction in the law of persons is this, that all men are either free, or slaves' (*Institutes* 1.9). Justinian explains: 'Slavery is an institution of the law of nations [it was common to the whole known world at the time and not a specifically Roman institution, though the Roman law, of course, was adapted to accommodate it] whereby one man is made the property of another, contrary to natural right' (*Institutes* 1.3.2).

A man was either born a slave, or became one. He was born a slave if his mother was a slave; he became a slave by the law of nations, under which captives, who would normally be killed, became slaves if their lives were spared, or by the law of Rome. The Roman law did not produce slaves in bulk like the

law of nations, but laid down specific circumstances, in which
individuals became slaves, for example thieves caught red-
handed, evaders of military service, insolvent debtors, freed
slaves who were grossly ungrateful to their patrons and free
men who fraudulently sold themselves as slaves. Two other
modes were abolished by Justinian – Hadrian had allowed
convicts sentenced to death, the mines or the arena to be
spared as slaves, and a freewoman who co-habited with a
slave against the wishes of the slave's owner could be enslaved
after a magistrate's order to that effect.

Slavery was a status, and so would normally be for life.
There was no idea of a period of slavery, as a punishment for
instance, but just as one could change status for the worse by
changing downwards into slavery, so one could change for
the better by moving upwards in society out of the ranks of
the slaves. The means was manumission: the manumitted
slave became a freedman (*libertinus*). Generally a slave could
become a freedman by buying his freedom with his *peculium*
(that is by saving up his pocket money – in strict theory a
slave, having no rights, could own no property, but from
quite early times they seem to have been allowed pocket
money, and indeed skilled men could earn good wages.
Though in the eyes of the law this belonged to the slave's
owner, relations between slave and owner were often good
enough for the slave to keep what he earned for himself) or
earn it by service. Early modes of manumission were formal:
a master could bring a slave for enrolment as a freedman at the
quinquennial census, free him by *vindicta* (a legal fiction
involving a formal claim of liberty) or by his will. This last
was the most popular method, as it ensured grateful mourners
at one's funeral. (The Romans liked to think they would have
a good send-off to the next world.) This method was the only
one which allowed conditions to be attached to a gift of
freedom. Until the condition was fulfilled the slave was not

freed, but was in an intermediate state known as *statuliber*, whereby, although still strictly a slave, he was protected from many of the indignities of slavery.

Informal methods of manumission appeared later. These were not strictly in accord with the *ius civile* but were recognized by the Praetors – pronouncing the slave free before five witnesses (for example at a party), inviting him to one's dinner table as a freedman, or by letter. Eventually so many slaves were being freed, many of them with bad characters, that Augustus, who was worried about dilution of the racial stock of Rome by intermarriage, introduced statutory restrictions in the Lex Fufia Caninia (2 B.C.) and Lex Aelia Sentia (A.D. 4). Slaves freed informally or outside the scope of this latter statute did not become freedmen but only *in libertate* or, after A.D. 19, Junian Latins (an intermediate condition from which full freedom could be achieved by a further manumission observing all necessary formalities, or by good works). The statute also created a degraded class of *dedeticii*. Gaius says:

The Lex Aelia Sentia provides that slaves who have had to be punished by their masters by being put in chains or branded, or have been questioned about misdeeds under torture and found guilty, or have been condemned to fight in the arena with men or beasts, or who have been put into a gladiatorial school or imprisoned, shall, if subsequently manumitted, whether by the same or by another master, become *dedeticii*. (*Institutes* 1.13)

Such men would never improve that status, nor were they allowed within a hundred miles of Rome, on pain of re-enslavement which would be permanent.

Justinian repealed the Lex Junia Norbana and Lex Aelia Sentia and abolished the status of *dedeticii*.

(ii) *Potestas*

Gaius says that there is another division in the law of persons 'for some are *sui iuris* (independent) and others are *alieni iuris* (dependent upon another)'.

Slaves are in the *potestas* (power) of their masters. This is an institution of the law of all nations, for masters always have power of life and death over their slaves, and whatever a slave acquires he acquired for his master. But at the present time, neither Roman citizens nor any other persons subject to the rule of the Roman people are allowed to treat their slaves with excessive harshness, for it is laid down in a Constitution of the late Emperor Antoninus of Blessed Memory that anyone who without cause kills his own slave is just as amenable to the law as he who kills another's. Even excessive severity on the part of masters is restrained by another Constitution of the same Emperor, for on being consulted by certain provincial governors about slaves who took refuge in the temples of the gods or at the statues of Emperors, he ordered that masters who show intolerable savagery are to be forced to sell their slaves to other owners. These enactments are just, for we ought not to abuse our lawful rights: this is the same principle by which prodigals are restrained from misuse of their own property.

Children whom we beget in civil marriage are also in our *potestas*. The right is peculiar to Roman citizens, for scarcely any other men have such power over their sons as we have. The late blessed Emperor Hadrian indicated as much in his Edict concerning those who petitioned him for citizenship for themselves and their children. Nor has it escaped me that the Galatians regarded their children as being in the *potestas* of their parents. (*Institutes*, 48; 50–53; 55)

(iii) *Tutors*

The Roman head of a household thus had *potestas* not only over his slaves, but also over his children, male and female. The head of the household was the *paterfamilias*, his son in power being a *filiusfamilias*. The son became *sui iuris* when his father died, but if that occurred before the son became of age, he had to have a tutor, whose function was to make good his lack of experience in legal matters. To be a tutor was regarded as a most solemn public duty, which the person nominated (usually by will of the deceased *paterfamilias*) was obliged to take on and from which he would be excused only in certain well-defined circumstances. The main duties of a tutor to a minor were to administer the ward's property to the best advantage and to supplement his legal incapacity when necessary. Without his tutor's authority a ward could not validly take any legal step which might cause him disadvantage. The arrangement ended when the ward became of age, when there was a settling of accounts under pain of grave penalties for a tutor who had acted with anything less than the strictest propriety.

A second, quaint form of tutorship existed in the early law – the perpetual tutelage of women, under which all women *sui iuris* and regardless of age were required to have a tutor. The reason was the protection of their property, over which they had little real control in the early law. Again, the tutor made good his ward's lack of legal capacity, but in this instance the appointment did not end at a given age. Gaius says that the early lawyers regarded women as being of a frivolous and unbusinesslike turn of mind and thus in need of this sort of protection, but the institution was in decay in his day and he said that

hardly any valid argument seems to exist for women of full age being in tutorship. That which is commonly accepted, namely that they are especially liable to be deceived in business owing to their instability of judgement and that therefore in fairness to themselves they should be subject to the authority of a tutor, seems more specious than true. Nowadays women of full age conduct their own affairs and the interposing of their tutor's authority is often merely a matter of form, so

much so that the tutor is often compelled by the Praetor to give his
authority even against his will. (*Institutes* 1.190)

As early as the Twelve Tables (451 B.C.) the Vestal Virgins
were exempted from the need to have tutors, but the real
decline of the institution can be traced from the Leges Juliae
et Papia Poppaea which freed married women from tutelage
when they had had three children (four in the case of freed-
women). This *ius trium liberorum* came to be conferred on certain
individuals who were not strictly qualified, as for example
when Augustus conferred it upon Livia, and eventually (A.D.
410) all women were presumed to have this 'right'.

Tutors should be distinguished from curators. A curator was
appointed to care for the insane and look after their property
for them (*cura furiosi*). In such circumstances a curator usually
had much more direct control over the person and property
in his care. Notorious squanderbugs and loose-livers could
also be subjected to curatorship (*cura prodigi*) until restored to
sobriety and sound morals.

(iv) *Married women*

The special status of married women, which arose from the
combination of what was in many ways a male-dominated law
with the rules of *potestas* and *manus*, gave rise to a number of
problems, as can be seen for example in Justinian's discussion
of the law of defamation (see pp. 158–85 below). He also says:
'A civil law marriage is contracted by Roman citizens who
are united according to law, males having reached the age of
puberty (14) and females being of marriageable age (12)
whether they be *sui iuris* or in power, provided that children
in power must have the consent of the *paterfamilias*' (*Institutes*
1.10.pr.) and the intention to live together as husband and wife.
Only this element distinguished informal marriages from concubinage.

A civil law marriage created a relationship known as *manus*, which arose in early law when the marriage was celebrated in particular ceremonial forms known as *confarreatio* and *coemptio*, but these were virtually obsolete by the time of Gaius. No ceremony of any sort was strictly necessary, as marriage was contracted by consent. *Manus* however, arose by *usus* or continual cohabitation and could be prevented by *trinoctii absentia* – an absence of three nights preventing the husband as it were from virtually usucaping the wife (as to *usucapio*, see pp. 56–9 below).

Where *manus* arose the wife ceased to be a member of her own family and came under the *potestas* of her husband's *paterfamilias*, or if he were *sui iuris* she came into his *manus* (literally into his hands) and he had the power of a *paterfamilias* over her and she stood as a daughter to him. Her property passed to her husband or his *paterfamilias* and any children of the marriage were born into the *potestas* of the head of the household. As might be expected this archaic arrangement was superseded by the *liberum maritagium* or 'free' marriage – free in that no *manus* arose. This was, according to Lee, the virtually universal type of arrangement in the classical age and was a relationship of

remarkable freedom. Marriage per se did not affect a transfer of the wife's property to the husband or give him any right of administration. She retained her contractual freedom, except that she could not make a gift to her husband any more than he could to her. This was one reason why it was of importance to fix the moment at which marriage took place. As the wife controlled her own property, so in law (it was thought) she was expected to provide for her own maintenance. It was not her husband's business to provide for her needs. (R. W. Lee , *The Elements of Roman Law*, 66)

This independence of the wife and lack of husband's rights to her property led to the institution of the marriage settlement or dowry (*dos*), but this never became legally necessary to marriage, though it was always good evidence that the parties intended marriage rather than concubinage. A particularly important result of a 'free marriage', however, was that the wife was not transferred from one *potestas* to another, but remained a member of her own family, subject to her own *paterfamilias*, or, if she were *sui iuris* and so under tutorship, she remained so despite the marriage until the perpetual tutelage of women became obsolete.

PROPERTY (*Res Mancipi and Usucapio*)

Just as people were classified by the Roman lawyers, so also, in various ways, was property. The *Institutes* of both Gaius and Justinian devote a good deal of space to classifications of property, dividing things into, for example, those subject to divine or human right, things corporeal and incorporeal (Gaius); and things common to all mankind, or subject to private, public, corporate or no ownership (Justinian). However, one of the divisions which had extensive legal implications was the classical distinction (abolished by Justinian) into things of which ownership had to be formally transferred (*res mancipi*) and things which could be transferred without special formality (*res nec mancipi*). Gaius tells us that *res mancipi* were the following: 'Italic land and houses on it; slaves and animals that are commonly broken to draught or burden and rustic praedial servitudes' (certain rights such as rights of way which one acquired together with land by virtue of owning it) (*Institutes* 2.14a). Other things are *res nec mancipi*, though the division, it seems, is not always clear; for example:

The effect of the previous statement, that animals commonly broken to draught or burden are *res mancipi*, is disputed by some, because they are not broken in at once on birth. The writers of our school maintain that they are *res mancipi* as soon as they are born, but Nerva, Proculus and the other authorities of the opposing school hold that they become *res mancipi* only when they have actually been broken in, or if they cannot be broken in because of extreme wildness, that they become *res mancipi* when they reach the usual age for breaking in. (*Institutes* 2.15)

The view of Gaius and the Sabinian school eventually prevailed. This was no mere academic haggle, however. The citizen buying or selling property needed to know whether it was a *res mancipi* or *nec mancipi*, for, as Gaius says, in law there is an important difference between the two. He explains thus:

Res nec mancipi became the full property of another by mere delivery, provided that they are corporeal and thus admit of being delivered. Thus, if I deliver a garment, or some gold or silver to you, be it on account of a sale or gift or any other good cause, it becomes yours at once, provided of course that I am its owner. *Res mancipi*, on the other hand, are those things that need to be conveyed by *mancipatio*: that is why they are called *res mancipi*. But *cessio in iure* is also valid to transfer their ownership. (*Institutes* 2.19, 20, 22)

It is thought that *res mancipi* were those things which were of greatest significance to the rustic community of early Rome and that this is why the transfer of their ownership (ownership itself being a concept which the Romans regarded with particular reverence) should be required to be effected with all due ceremony and solemnity. *Mancipatio* was a ceremony peculiar to citizens and dating from a time before coined money was used, but which remained in a symbolic form long after coinage was introduced. The buyer and seller met together in the presence of five witnesses (symbolic of the five ancient tribes of Rome and representing the whole Roman people) and a sixth (the *libripens*), who held a pair of bronze scales. The buyer took hold of the object being transferred to him with one hand and a piece of bronze in the other and said aloud, 'I declare this slave (cow, or whatever) to be mine by the law of the Quirites and purchased by me with this piece of bronze upon these bronze scales.' He then struck the scales with the bronze (symbolic of weighing it out) and handed it to the transferor.

Cessio in iure was a collusive version of a court action claiming ownership, which was compromised by the parties. Both ceremonies required formal words to be uttered and only the correct usage of those words could create the unique bond of ownership that could exist only between a Roman citizen and a *res mancipi*.

Quite clearly, however, they were grossly cumbersome procedures and wholly inappropriate to the bustling commercial society that Rome subsequently became. A new means therefore had to be found to protect those who did not, for whatever reason, but often simply for lack of time, use these formal modes to transfer *res mancipi*. That means was *usucapio*, a method of acquiring ownership by long possession. If a slave or cow were simply transferred without formality, no ownership would pass to the transferee. In the eyes of the law it remained with the transferor, but the Twelve Tables provided that if the slave or cow were continuously possessed by the transferee for a whole year (or two years in the case of immovables) ownership would be acquired at the end of that period. Long possession (*usucapio*) could thus make good the lack of due formality at the time of transfer.

When Justinian abolished the distinction between *res mancipi* and *res nec mancipi*, ownership of any item of property could be transferred simply by handing over the thing. The original *raison d'être* of *usucapio* thus disappeared, but it remained in use to enable the law to treat as practically owner anyone who was in possession of property as owner but without legal title, and to recognize him as fully owner after the lapse of the necessary time.

Simply to lay down a period of time to elapse which would transform the transferee's possession into full legal ownership, while going some way to mitigate the harshness of the legal requirement of formality, still left serious problems unsolved, particularly if the possessor who was in the course of perfecting his title by effluxion of time lost that possession before the necessary period had elapsed.

If *A* sold a slave, cow or any other *res mancipi* to *B* and on receipt of the purchase money simply handed it over without *mancipatio* or *cessio in iure*, *A* still retained ownership in the eyes of the civil law. At first therefore if he brought a formal action to recover the thing *(vindicatio)*, *B* had no answer to his claim. The Praetor's Edict, however, came to *B*'s aid in granting him the defence that he had the thing because it had been sold and handed over to him *(exceptio rei venditae et traditae)*. Once this was available, *B* had a good answer to the claim of the vendor or to anyone claiming through him. He still remained vulnerable to claims by third parties if he lost possession – for example, someone might enter upon a farm which he had bought and was usucaping, and refuse to give up possession. He could not bring the *vindicatio*, since that involved an assertion that he sued as owner in the eyes of the civil law (which he was not). His vendor *(A)* might be prevailed upon to bring such action (he was, after all, still technically owner) and put *B* back into possession, but despite the Roman traditions of honourable conduct, he might not see why he should be so bothered, gratuitously; or he might be far away, or untraceable. Eventually, the Praetor came to *B*'s aid here too, in the *actio Publiciana*. This action was probably introduced by the urban Praetor Publicius who was in office in the latter years of the Republic, not long before the time of Augustus. This new action proceeded upon the basis that *B* could not yet bring a *vindicatio*, but that he would be able to do so in the normal course of events when sufficient time had elapsed for him to complete *usucapio*. The judge was accordingly to give his decision in favour of *B* if satisfied that he had been properly in possession and that he would have become civil law owner if he had held the thing for the necessary period.

ACTIONS

Primitive legal 'systems' are usually not systems at all but simply a number of remedies available for certain types of wrongs. Thus, in early English law there was no thought of an all-embracing law which would, as we now assume, provide protection for the citizen's rights of all sorts, but rather a number of writs which were available to set in motion a selection of formalized actions to remedy certain specific ills. If the injustice suffered fell outside the scope of the writs, the would-be litigant had no remedy in the law. Eventually the old forms of action disappeared, being superseded by the approach that the law should provide a remedy for anyone whose rights had been infringed and not be hampered by a procedure which could operate only in a number of defined instances. The old lawyers looked first to the repertoire of set remedies; we now look first to the right.

A similar development is to be seen in the Roman law. In its earliest days, procedure was far more important than the substantive law, and the *legis actiones* provided a strictly formal process, which had to be rigidly adhered to, to deal with certain sorts of legal wrongs. The Praetors, however, through their control of the granting of remedies, were able in effect to extend the scope of the law by granting remedies where none had existed previously. As Nicholas[1] observes: 'By creating a new form of action or extending an old form to new facts he could in effect create new rights. In form there was

1. *An Introduction to Roman Law*, p. 20.

merely a new remedy, in substance there was new law.' The
old *legis actiones* however, were restricted to five ritual forms,
so it was only after the reform of procedure by the introduction of the more flexible formulary system that the Praetor
began to have a really significant influence upon the extension
and development of the law to meet new requirements.
Exactly how and when this system replaced the archaic *legis
actiones* is uncertain. The Lex Aebutia is the statute which
some say introduced it – though it more probably simply
sanctioned existing practices; but despite its great importance
its exact date is unknown. The general view, however, is that
it must have been passed towards the end of the second century B.C. What is clear is that the new forms of procedure were
in use by then.

This new procedure is known to us as the Formulary System. It remained in use throughout the Classical period of
Roman law, despite the great changes which occurred,
because its simplicity and flexibility enabled it to meet the
demands placed upon it. The essence of the system was that
each action had an appropriate form, which was set in motion
by a formula, or statement of the cause of action. Each formula was made up from a number of sections which were
made up according to a number of general patterns but were
flexible enough to enable the gist of a case to be set out
clearly and concisely. 'Thus if there had been a contract of
sale *(emptio venditio)* and the seller refused to deliver what he
had sold, the buyer had an action on the purchase *(actio empti)*,
and conversely if the buyer refused to pay the price, the
seller had an action on the sale *(actio venditi)*; and each action
had an appropriate formula in which the issue was defined.'
Thus defined, it was presented to the court and the judge
(iudex).

Turning now to the particular subjects discussed by Justinian in those parts of the *Digest* included in this volume, a

plaintiff who had been injured directly by the negligence of the defendant would sue him by means of the *actio legis Aquiliae*. This action was at first, however, only available in a relatively small number of cases falling directly within the strictly construed words of the Lex Aquilia itself. For example, the use of the word *occidere* (to kill) in Chapter One of the Lex, which imposes liability for destroying property, was construed as meaning that the Lex applied only where the killing was done directly by the person of the accused, or with a weapon held by him. The early lawyers, however, quite soon interpreted the Lex as applying also where a killing was done by poisoning, but even the extended rule was understood as applying only where the damage was done *corpore corpori* (that is by the wrongdoer's body to the damaged thing). Similarly *rumpere* (to smash) in Chapter 3 was at first narrowly interpreted, but later extended to include any sort of material damage, including liability for *damnum emergens* (loss due to extrinsic circumstances, such as the killing of one horse of a pair, or one acrobat from a troupe) and *lucrum cessans* (an expected profit which the owner has been making). Perhaps the most significant development of this branch of the law through juristic interpretation arose from their attitude to *iniuria* (unlawfulness). Originally this requirement of the Lex Aquilia probably meant that the defendant should be liable for death or damage directly caused by the body to the body in circumstances where he was not acting *iure*, that is in pursuance of some right. The *Digest* lists cases where a defence is afforded by self-defence, public office or private right. It is likely, however, as Professor Lawson suggests,[2] that quite soon the defendant could plead that although he had killed or injured the plaintiff's property, he had done so under circumstances in which he could not have acted otherwise, and so was not to blame. By introducing this element of fault and

2. F. H. Lawson, *Negligence in the Civil Law*, 15.

moving away from earlier notions of strict liability (liability without proof of the defendant's fault by the plaintiff), the jurists created a law of potentially great flexibility and adaptability to an apparently infinite range of circumstance, which has enabled the law of the Lex Aquilia to be applied to this day in negligence cases in jurisdictions with a Roman law foundation.

Beyond these adjustments by interpretation the extension of the law was in the hands of the Praetors, who might give or withhold rights of action in analogous circumstances especially through the *actio utilis* and *actio in factum*. Buckland explains thus:[3]

The law applied only where the damage was by the body to the body, *corpore corpori*. The Praetor gave an action, *utilis* or *in factum* in cases not within this conception, where it was not by but to the body, as by throwing grain into a river. It might not be harmed, but in effect it was destroyed. So too where it was to, but not by, the body, as by putting poison where a slave was likely to take it, but not actually administering it. So too where it was neither, as by opening a stable door so that animals escaped and were lost. It is easy to see that these lines might be difficult to draw. There is no great difference between mixing the seed in the bag, which gives the direct action, and sowing false seed, which does not. The line between actually administering poison and facilitating the taking might be rather fine.

In some cases the *actio utilis* was given; in others an *actio in factum*. Gaius makes it *utilis* wherever it was not *corpore* (i.e. damage by the body): the *Institutes* [of Justinian] say that if it was not *corpore* or *corpori* (i.e. to the body) the action was *in factum*, which would make it *utilis* if it was *corpore* but not *corpori*. But the texts in the *Digest* do not conform to any rule. Even the direct action is given in cases which seem to be more appropriate to one of the others, and as between these, no logical scheme is attainable, perhaps because the question was one of procedure and practically obsolete under Justinian.

3. Buckland, *A Textbook of Roman Law*, p. 589.

THE ROMAN LAW OF DELICTS

❖

THE selected passages from the *Digest* which follow make up
the Roman law of delicts. The term 'delict' is used in many
legal systems, notably nowadays for example in Scotland, to
indicate what in England we call torts. A tort is extremely
difficult to define in a way satisfactory to the jurist, but easy
enough to illustrate in general terms. Even so, it is usually
explained more by reference to what it is not than to what it
is. It is said to be a civil (that is non-criminal) legal wrong
which arises other than from contract. In contract cases, rights
to compensation arise from the breach of the agreement which
is the essence of contract, but in tort cases one is faced with
situations where the parties are brought into a legal relationship irrespective of agreement. This branch of the law concerns
itself with negligence (as for example when X runs down Y
because he is not taking as much care as he should – the care
that a reasonable man would take) and nuisance, libel and
slander, assault, battery and trespass. These wrongs are also
the province of the Scottish (and the Roman) law of delicts,
based on the second of the three famous precepts of Ulpian:
'*Juris praecepta sunt haec: honeste vivere, alterum non laedere, suum
cuique tribuere.*'[1] Explaining the application of this maxim
Erskine says in his *Institute of the Law of Scotland*, 'every one
who has the exercise of reason, and so can distinguish between
right and wrong, is naturally obliged to make up the damage

1. Quoted by Justinian, *Institutes* 1, 1, 3: *Digest* 1, 1, 10. 'The maxims
of the law are these: to live honestly, to harm no one, and to give
everyone his due.'

befalling his neighbour from a wrong committed by himself. Wherefore every fraudulent contrivance, or unwarrantable act, by which another suffers damage, or runs the hazard of it, subjects the delinquent to reparation.'[2]

More recently the late Dean Wright explained the development of the maxim in the English law of torts as follows:

Arising out of the various and ever-increasing clashes of the activities of persons living in a common society, carrying on business in competition with fellow members of that society, owning property which may in any of a thousand ways affect the person or property of others – in short doing all the things that constitute modern living – there must of necessity be losses, or injuries of many kinds sustained as a result of the activities of others. The purpose of the law of torts is to adjust these losses and to afford compensation for injuries sustained by one person as the result of the conduct of another ... The study of the law of torts is, therefore, a study of the extent to which the law will shift the losses sustained in modern society from the person affected to the shoulder of him who caused the loss or, more realistically in many fields, to the insurance companies who are increasingly covering the many risks involved in the conduct of business and individual activities.[3]

As to the scope of the law of delicts or torts, apart from the reference to insurance, Wright's view might just as well have been written by a Roman jurist about the Roman law of delicts. There was however, a major difference of purpose and of approach between the Roman and the modern law of delicts, for whereas the object of modern delictal actions is to compensate the sufferer and, so far as money can, to put him back into the position in which he would have been had the defendant not committed the delict, the object of the Roman law was to penalize the wrongdoer. The earliest actions were probably an attempt to regularize what might otherwise have

2. Erskine, *Institute* 3, 1, 13.
3. Wright, *Cases on the Law of Torts*, p. 1.

become a vendetta and to substitute a legal proceeding for personal vengeance, and this attitude of legalized self-help can be clearly seen in a number of examples in the early law of the Twelve Tables. At its simplest it provides for a killing, for example of an armed thief, to be guiltless. Similarly, before money penalties became the rule, a manifest (red-handed) thief still had to be brought before the court to be formally assigned to the plaintiff for the wreaking of his vengeance. He had thus to restrain himself until that stage had been gone through. In personal injury cases, where the guilt of the defendant was not necessarily so obvious and had to be established in court, he would therefore be assigned to the plaintiff for retaliation, but not just as the plaintiff saw fit, only for retaliation in kind – an eye for an eye, a tooth for a tooth and so on. In other cases, money penalties without the option of vengeance soon became the rule, and in later law, physical vengeance, which was no less barbarous for being awarded by a court order, virtually disappeared, being replaced by pecuniary awards. It is tempting to think thereafter in modern compensatory terms, but it must be remembered that Roman delictal actions began by being legalized vengeance and that they retained their penal character: the sum assessed tends to be double or four times the value of the thing lost or damaged. Furthermore, if two or more persons committed a delict together, each was fully liable for the whole penalty. The law was not concerned that the plaintiff recovered his loss many times over – after all, no blame attached to him – but was much more concerned to see that each wrongdoer was fully penalized.

To the Romans, delicts could be of two kinds, public (which we call crimes – thus the Romans cast this net wider than we do now) and private (our law of torts). These two branches of law were not, of course, mutually exclusive, and the same event might well give rise to liability to more than one action.

The Romans, so given to dividing all manner of things into categories, divided delicts into four classes for purposes of legal exposition. The three oldest were the delicts of theft (*furtum*), damage (*damnum iniuria datum*) and insult (*iniuria*). They were subsequently much expanded and developed by the Praetors and by the jurists. The fourth, robbery (*rapina*), was a later addition, the creation of which was attributed to the Praetor Lucullus, who introduced the *actio vi bonorum raptorum* in his Edict of 76 B.C. However, although that Edict was indeed issued in that year, it is now the preferred view that the delict *rapina* had probably developed gradually over a considerable period, though the history of the action is obscure. Lucullus probably brought it to prominence as a firm measure to meet the needs of his time when law and order were in serious decline.

The passages following are all examples of civil wrongs, for in the *Digest* the public delicts or crimes are expounded quite separately – as indeed they are by our textbook writers today. They have been chosen rather than, say, the law of contracts, not only because they are concerned with situations which in many instances are just like today's, but also because the facts of many of the cases discussed are simple and graphic and thus create immediate mental pictures in a way in which discussions of points of 'lawyer's law' do not, and for the lay reader, cannot. Some cases, however, such as those concerned with runaway slaves, defamed married women or fraudulent tutors, and discussions of the type of legal proceeding available to meet certain circumstances, cannot make sense without some knowledge of the background law, and for this reason that necessary background has already been outlined; but most of the cases discussed arose out of everyday events in the life of the thriving and cosmopolitan communities of the Roman world. Rome not only gave her law to the whole of known civilization: she was also a great centre for trade with all corners of the world and a city where all sorts of foreigners came into contact with the people at home. One can sense this world in Ostia Antica and in Pompeii; and here in the *Digest* we have a fascinating picture of the ordinary life of the Roman world which, apart from Petronius – and he gives nothing like the wealth of lively detail – is so little documented. Here is a glimpse of everyday hurlyburly and commonplace things, accidents in the street, ball games, clothes taken to the cleaners; the picture takes in town and country, for we see the man whose oven causes his neighbour's house to burn down as well as the farmer whose stubble-burning destroys the next man's vineyard; there are dwellers in cool villas and the occupants of densely-packed tenements; deals in shops, honest, unfortunate and crooked; thieves and brawling; defrauded workmen and all manner of ramifications of deals with all sorts of and conditions of men. Tinkers, tailors, soldiers, sailors, rich men, poor men, beggarmen and thieves – they were with the Romans then, just as they are with us now.

THE DIGEST OF
ROMAN LAW

THEFT, RAPINE, DAMAGE
AND INSULT

CONCERNING THE LEX AQUILIA

◆

1. (ULPIAN) The Lex Aquilia took away the force of all earlier laws which dealt with unlawful damage – the Twelve Tables and others alike – and it is no longer necessary to refer to them. The Lex Aquilia is a plebiscite, the enactment of which by the plebs was procured by the tribune Aquilius.

2. (GAIUS) The first chapter of the Lex Aquilia provides as follows: 'If anyone kills unlawfully a slave or servant-girl belonging to someone else, or a four-footed beast of the class of cattle, let him be condemned to pay the owner the highest value that the property had attained in the preceding year.' And next it is provided that the action should be for double the value if the defendant denied his liability. It thus appears that the statute treats equally our slaves and our four-footed cattle which are kept in herds, such as sheep, goats, horses, mules and asses. But it has been questioned whether pigs should be included amongst cattle, and Labeo rightly holds that they are. A dog, however, does not fall within this class and it is much more apparent that wild beasts such as bears, lions and panthers are not cattle either. But elephants and camels are, as it were, 'mixed', for they serve as draught animals; but they are by nature wild and accordingly should be within the scope of the first chapter.

3. (ULPIAN) If a slave or servant-girl is wrongfully killed, the Lex Aquilia applies; but it is rightly added that the killing

must be unlawful, for killing alone is not enough – it must have been done unlawfully.

4. (GAIUS) Accordingly if I kill your slave who is lying in ambush to rob me, I shall go free, for natural reason permits a person to defend himself against danger. The law of the Twelve Tables permits one to kill a thief caught in the night, provided one gives evidence of the fact by shouting aloud, but someone may only kill a person caught in such circumstances at any other time if he defends himself with a weapon, though only if he provides evidence by shouting.

5. (ULPIAN) If someone kills anyone else who is trying to go for him with a sword, he will not be deemed to have killed unlawfully; and if for fear of death someone kills a thief, there is no doubt that he will not be liable under the Lex Aquilia. But if, although he could have arrested him, he preferred to kill him, the better opinion is that he should be deemed to have acted unlawfully (*iniuria*), and therefore he will also be liable under the Lex Cornelia.

We must here of course not take *iniuria* as meaning some sort of insult, as it indicates in the *actio iniuriarum*, but as indicating something done illegally, that is, contrary to the law – as for example if one kills wrongfully. Thus, although from time to time the action under the Lex Aquilia and the action for insult concur, there will in such a case be two assessed heads of damages, one for wrongful harm and one for insult. Therefore we interpret *iniuria* for present purposes as including damage caused in a blameworthy fashion, even by one who did not intend the harm. And accordingly the question is asked whether there is an action under the Lex Aquilia if a lunatic causes damage. Pegasus says there is not, for he asks how there can be any accountable fault in him who is out of his mind; and he is undoubtedly right. Therefore the Aquilian action will fail in such a case, just as it fails if an animal has caused damage or if a tile has fallen; and the same must be said if an infant has caused damage, though Labeo says that if the child were over seven years of age he could be liable under the Lex Aquilia in just the same way as he could be liable for theft. I think this is correct, provided the child were able to distinguish between right and wrong.

If a teacher kills or wounds a slave during a lesson, is he liable under the Lex Aquilia for having done unlawful damage? Julian writes that a man who had put out a pupil's eye in the course of instruction was held liable under the Lex. There is all the more reason therefore for saying the same if he kills him. Julian also puts this case: a shoemaker, he says, struck with a last at the neck of a boy (a freeborn youngster) who was learning under him, because he had done badly what he had been teaching him, with the result that the boy's eye was knocked out. On such facts, says Julian, the action for insult does not lie because he struck him not with intent to insult, but in order to correct and teach him; he wonders whether there is an action for breach of the contract for his services as a teacher, since a teacher only has the right to administer reasonable chastisement, but I have no doubt that action can be brought against him under the Lex Aquilia,

6. (PAUL) for excessive brutality on the part of a teacher is blameworthy.

7. (ULPIAN) And in this action the father will recover the amount of his loss of prospective profit from his son's services, of which he is deprived through the eye being damaged, and also the expenses incurred for medical attention.

Now we must accept 'killing' to include the cases where the assailant hit his victim with a sword or a stick or other weapon, or did him to death with his hands (if for example he strangled him), or kicked him with his foot or butted him, or any other such ways. But if one who is overloaded unreasonably throws down his burden and kills a slave, the Aquilian action lies; for it was within his own judgement not to load himself thus. For even if someone slips and crushes another man's slave with his load, Pegasus maintains that he is liable under the Lex Aquilia provided he overloaded himself unreasonably or negligently walked through a slippery place. Thus if someone does damage through being pushed by somebody else, Proculus writes that neither is liable under the Lex: the one who pushed is not liable because he did not kill, nor is the one who was pushed because he did not do the damage unlawfully. According to this view an action *in factum* will be given against the one who pushed. If a man kills another in the *colluctatio*[1] or in the *pancratium*,[2] or in a boxing-match (provided the one kills the other in a public bout) the Lex Aquilia does not apply because the damage is seen to have been done in the cause of glory and valour and not for the sake of inflicting unlawful harm; but this does not apply in the case of a slave, because the custom is that only freeborn people compete in this way. It does, however, apply where a son in power is hurt. Clearly, if someone wounds a contestant who has thrown in the towel the Lex Aquilia will apply, as it will also if he kills a slave who is not in the contest, except if he has been entered for a fight by his master – then the action fails.

But if someone gives a light blow to a sickly slave and he dies from it, Labeo rightly says that he is liable under the Lex Aquilia, for different things are lethal for different people.

Celsus says it matters a great deal whether one kills directly or brings about a cause of death, because he who furnishes an indirect cause of death is not liable to an Aquilian action, but to an *actio in factum*, wherefore he refers to a man who administered poison instead of medicine and says that he thereby brought about a cause of death, in the same way as one who holds out a sword to a madman; and such a man is not liable under the Lex but to an *actio in factum*.

But if a man throws another off a bridge Celsus says that, regardless of whether he is killed by the impact or merely drowns at once, or whether he perishes from exhaustion because he is overcome by the force of the current, there is liability under the Lex Aquilia, just as if one dashes a child against a rock. Proculus says that if a doctor operates negligently on a slave an action will lie either on the contract for his services or under the Lex Aquilia.

8. And the law is just the same if one misuses a drug, or if, having operated efficiently, the aftercare is neglected: the wrongdoer will not go free, but is deemed to be guilty of negligence. Furthermore if a mule-driver cannot control his mules because he is inexperienced and as a result they run down somebody's slave, he is generally said to be liable on grounds of negligence. It is the same if it is because of weakness that he cannot hold back his mules – and it does not seem unreasonable that weakness should be deemed negligence, for no one should undertake a task in which he knows, or ought to know, that his weakness may be a danger to others. The legal position is just the same for a person who through inexperience or weakness cannot control a horse he is riding.

9. Labeo makes this distinction if a midwife gives a drug from which the woman dies: if she administers it with her own hands it would appear that she killed; but if she gave it to the woman for her to take it herself an action *in factum* must be granted. This opinion is correct, for she provided a cause of death rather than killed. If someone administers a drug to anyone by force or persuasion, either in a drink or by injection, or rubs him with a poisonous potion, he is liable under the Lex Aquilia; and Neratius says that if a man starves a slave to death he is liable to an *actio in factum*.

If when my slave is out riding you scare his horse so that he is thrown into a river and dies as a result, Ofilius writes that an *actio in factum* must be given, in just the same way as when my slave is lured into an ambush by one man and killed by another. But if a slave is killed by people throwing javelins by way of sport, the Aquilian action lies. On the other hand if when other people were already throwing javelins in a field a slave walked across the same field the Aquilian action fails, because he should not make his way at an inopportune time across a field where javelin throwing is being practised. However, anyone who deliberately aims at him is liable under the Lex Aquilia,

10. (PAUL) for playing dangerous games is blameworthy conduct.

11. (ULPIAN) Further, Mela writes that, when some people were playing with a ball, one of them hit it hard and it knocked the hands of a barber, with the result that the throat of a slave, whom the barber was shaving, was cut by the jerking of the razor. In which of the parties does the fault lie? – for it is he who is liable under the Lex Aquilia. Proculus says the blame is the barber's, and surely, if he was doing shaving in a place where people customarily played games or where there was much going to and fro, the blame will be imputed to him; but it is no bad point in reply that if someone entrusts himself to a barber who has his chair in a dangerous place he has only himself to blame for his own misfortune.

If one man holds a slave while another kills him, he who did the holding will be liable to an *actio in factum* because he furnished a cause of death. But if several people do a slave to death, let us see whether they are all liable as for killing. If it is clear from whose blow he perished, that person is liable for killing; but if it is not clear, Julian says that all the assailants are liable as if they had all killed; and if the action is brought against only one of them, the others are not released from liability, for under the Lex Aquilia what one pays does not lessen what is due from another, as it is a penal law.

Celsus writes that if one attacker inflicts a mortal wound on a slave and another person later finishes him off, he who struck the earlier blow will not be liable for a killing, but for wounding, because he actually perished as the result of another wound. The later assailant will be held liable because he did the killing. It seems thus to Marcellus and it is the more likely.

If several people throw down a beam and thereby crush a slave, it seemed right to the ancient jurists that they should all be liable under the Lex Aquilia. Again, Proculus gave an opinion that the Aquilian action lies against him who, though he was not in charge of a dog, annoyed it and thus caused it to bite someone; but Julian says the Lex Aquilia only applies to this extent, that it applies to him who had the dog on a lead and caused it to bite someone; otherwise, if he were not holding it, an *actio in factum* must be brought.

The action on the Lex Aquilia is available to the '*erus*', that is, the owner.

If wrongful damage is done to a slave whom I am returning to you because he has some serious defect which rescinds the contract for his sale to me, Julian says an action under the Lex Aquilia has accrued to me, but that I must cede it to you when I begin the restoration of the slave to you.

But if a slave is in the service of one who is not his owner, but who wrongly though in good faith believes that he is, is the Aquilian action available to him? It seems rather that an *actio in factum* will be given. Julian says that a person to whom clothes have been lent cannot proceed under the Lex Aquilia if they are torn, but that the action is available to the owner. Julian also discusses whether those granted the use and enjoyment of the produce of another's property have the action; but I think that in such circumstances it is rather the *actio utilis* that should be given.

12. (PAUL) But if the true owner wounds or kills a slave in whom I have a usufruct,[3] I should be given an action against him on the analogy of the Lex Aquilia, according to the value of my usufruct, so that even the part of the year before my

usufruct was created should be brought into account in making the valuation.

13. (ULPIAN) For an injury to himself a free man has on his own account an *actio utilis* after the manner of the Aquilian action. He cannot have the direct action under the Lex because no one is deemed to be the owner of his own limbs. The owner has a direct action on account of a runaway slave.

Julian writes that if a free man acts in the honest belief that he is my slave, he is liable to me under the Lex Aquilia for any damage he does.

If a slave who is part of an unclaimed inheritance is killed, it is debated who can bring the Aquilian action, since no one is the owner of such a slave. Celsus says that the law meant any loss to be made good to the owner and that the inheritance is therefore deemed to be the owner. Accordingly the heir may sue when he has entered into his inheritance. If a slave left as a legacy is killed after the heir's entry into the inheritance, the legatee is competent to bring the action under the Lex Aquilia if he did not acknowledge his legacy after the slave's death; but if he refused his legacy, Julian says the consequence is that the action is available to the heir.

14. (PAUL) But if the heir himself kills the slave, it is said that an action must be given to the legatee against him.

15. (ULPIAN) From the opinion of Julian it follows that if a slave left as a legacy is killed before the heir enters upon his inheritance, the Aquilian action which has been acquired by the inheritance remains for the heir. But if the slave should be wounded before the entry of the heir, the action still remains in the inheritance, but it should be assigned to the legatee.

If a slave who has been mortally wounded afterwards has his death accelerated by the collapse of a house or by shipwreck or by some other sort of blow, no action can be brought for killing, but only as if he were wounded; but if he dies from a wound after he has been freed or alienated, Julian says an action can be brought for killing. These situations are so different for this reason: because the truth is that in the latter case he was killed by you when you were wounding him, which only became apparent later by his death; but in the former case whether or not he was killed was not clear because it was affected by the collapse of the house.

But if you order that a mortally wounded slave shall be freed and be your heir and then he dies, his heir cannot sue on the Lex Aquilia,

16. (MARCIANUS) because in this case matters had reached a point where an action cannot arise.

17. (ULPIAN) If a master kills his own slave he will be liable to a bona fide possessor or one who had accepted him as a pledge, in an *actio in factum*.

18. (PAUL) But if he who has accepted the slave as a pledge kills or wounds him, a right of action can arise under both the Lex Aquilia and the contract of pledge, though the plaintiff will have to be content with one or the other.

19. (ULPIAN) However, if someone kills a slave owned jointly with another, the Lex Aquilia applies to him; and it is the same if he wounded him,

20. (ULPIAN) of course, in proportion to the plaintiff's share of ownership.

21. (ULPIAN) As the measure of damages the Lex refers to 'Whatever was the highest value of the slave during that year'. This clause contains the mode of valuation of the damage that has been done. Now the year is reckoned backwards from the time when the slave was killed; but if he was mortally wounded and later died after a long interval, we shall reckon the year, according to Julian, from the time he was wounded, though Celsus writes to the contrary. But are we valuing only his body, how much it was worth when he

was killed, or rather how much it was worth to us that he should not be killed? We use this rule – that the valuation should be what he was worth to the plaintiff.

22. (PAUL) Thus, if you have killed a slave whom I have promised to hand over under a penalty, my benefit comes into account in the judgement. Furthermore, other heads of damage necessarily connected are taken into account, if (for example) someone kills one of a troupe of actors or musicians, or one of twins, or of a chariot team, or one of a pair of mules; for not only must a valuation be made of the object destroyed but it must also be borne in mind how much the value of the others has been lessened.

23. (ULPIAN) Therefore Neratius writes that if a slave who has been instituted as heir is killed, the value of the inheritance comes into the reckoning.

Julian says that if a slave is killed when it has been ordered that he should go free and become an heir, neither the substitute nor the statutory heir will secure by an action under the Lex Aquilia the value of the inheritance, which was not yet due to the slave himself; and this view is correct. Therefore he says that there should be an assessment only of the slave's market value, because this appears to be the only interest of the substitute. On the other hand I think that not even the slave's market value should be the measure of damages because, if the slave had become heir, he would also have become free. The same Julian writes further that if I should be instituted heir on the condition of freeing the slave Stichus and Stichus is killed after the testator's death, I can sue for the value of the inheritance in the assessment of my damages, for the condition failed because of the killing. But if he is killed in the testator's lifetime the valuation of the inheritance is not made because the highest valuation is calculated retrospectively. Julian also writes that the valuation of the dead slave is made as at that time in the preceding year when he was worth most; and accordingly if the thumb of a most valuable painter had been cut off beforehand and within a year of its loss he is killed, the Aquilian action lies and he must be valued at his price before he lost his skill together with his thumb. On the other hand in the case of killing a slave who had committed great embezzlements in running my affairs and whom I had resolved to examine by torture in order to drag out the names of his accomplices in dishonesty, Labeo writes very rightly that he must be valued according to my interest in detecting the frauds he had committed and not according to the value of the harm he had done. But if a worthy slave becomes a depraved character and is killed within a year his value will be calculated according to what he was worth before he changed his ways. In short we must say that all those useful things that made the slave worth more within the year in which he was killed are to be added to his value.

If a baby not yet a year old is killed, the better view is that this action will meet the case by referring the valuation to that part of the year for which he had lived.

It is settled that this action is given to heirs and other successors, but it will not be given against an heir or the other successors because it is penal – unless perchance the heir has been made richer as a result of the damage done.

If a slave is killed maliciously it is agreed that his owner can take action also under the Lex Cornelia; and if he shall already have sued under the Lex Aquilia the Cornelian action need not be judged first.

The Aquilian action lies for simple damages against a defendant who confesses, but for double against one who denies liability. If someone falsely confesses to killing a slave who is still alive and afterwards is ready to show that the slave is still alive, Julian writes that the Aquilian action no longer lies, even though he had confessed to killing; for an action on a confession only relieves the plaintiff from necessarily having to bring proof that the defendant killed the slave – it is still necessary that the slave must actually have been killed by someone or other.

24. (PAUL) This is more obvious in a case about a wounded slave, for if someone confesses to wounding when the slave was not hurt, what wound are we to value, or to what time shall we reckon back?

25. (ULPIAN) Accordingly if a slave has not been slain but has nevertheless died, the better view is that the defendant is not liable for the dead slave, even though he may have confessed.

If a procurator or tutor or curator or some such agent confesses to a wounding by their absent principal an *actio utilis* on the confession must be given against them. It must be noted that in this action which is given against the confessor the judge is appointed not to decide liability but only to assess the damages; for none of the elements of the judicial function are present in such cases of confession as these.

26. (PAUL) Just suppose that someone who has been summoned confesses to a killing and is prepared to pay the damages, but his opponent claims an excessive amount.

27. (ULPIAN) If a slave carries off and kills someone else's slave, both Julian and Celsus write that actions lie for both theft and wrongful damage. If a slave in common ownership, mine and yours, kills another slave of mine, the Lex Aquilia lies against you if he did it with your consent. Urseius reports that this was the opinion held by Proculus; but he says that if the slave did it without your consent, a noxal action[4] will not lie in case it might be in the power of the slave to decide which he might serve exclusively; and I think this is correct.

Again if a slave owned by you and me in common is killed by the slave of Titius, Celsus writes that if either of us sues he should recover the assessed value of his share, or noxal surrender will have to be made of the miscreant as a whole, because this solution is not susceptible of division.

The owner is held liable in respect of a slave who kills, but not a person whom he is serving in good faith; but it has been questioned whether he who has a runaway slave is liable on his account under the Lex Aquilia. Julian says he is liable and this is undoubtedly so, for even Marcellus agrees.

The second chapter of the Lex Aquilia has fallen into disuse.

In its third chapter the Lex Aquilia says: 'In the case of all other things apart from slaves or cattle that have been killed, if anyone does damage to another by wrongfully burning, breaking or spoiling his property, let him be condemned to pay to the owner whatever the damage shall prove to be worth in the next thirty days.'

If therefore someone does not kill, but burns, smashes or spoils a slave or beast, there is no doubt that action may be brought under these words of the Lex. Accordingly if you throw a lighted torch at my slave and singe him, you will be liable to me. Again, if you set fire to my orchard or my country house, I shall have the Aquilian action. If someone wished to burn down my tenement building and the fire spread to my neighbour's block of flats, he will be liable to my neighbour too. He will also be liable just the same to the tenants in respect of their property that is burnt.

If a tenant-farmer's stoker-slave drops asleep at the furnace and the house is burnt down Neratius says that the tenant must nevertheless make good the damage in accordance with the agreement in the contract of letting, if he was negligent in choosing his workers. But if one man lit the furnace but another watched it carelessly, will the one who lit it be liable? For he who watched it did nothing, while the one who lit it properly was not at fault. What is the answer? I think that an *actio utilis* lies just as much against the man who fell asleep at the furnace as against him who watched it negligently, nor can anyone say that he who fell asleep was only afflicted by a normal human failing, for it was his duty either to put out the fire or to take such care that it did not escape.

If you have an oven against a party wall will you be liable for wrongful damage? Proculus says there can be no action because there is no similar liability on the part of a man who has a fireplace, but I think it would be fairer for an *actio in factum* to be given if perchance the wall were burned down. On the other hand if you have not yet done me any damage but you have such a fire that I fear that you will cause me damage, I think your giving security against threatened damage should suffice.

Proculus says that when the slaves of a tenant-farmer have burned down the country house, the tenant is liable either on the contract of tenancy or under the Lex Aquilia, but with the privilege that the tenant is able to hand over the slaves for punishment. And if the case is decided in one of these actions the other cannot be brought in addition. But the position is thus only if the tenant-farmer was free of fault. On the other hand if he had culpable slaves he will be liable for resulting harm by reason of having such slaves. He writes that the same rule must apply also to the lodgers in a hostel.

If, when my bees had flown off to join yours, you burn them out, Celsus says the action on the Lex Aquilia lies.

The statute actually says '*ruperit*' (break or rend asunder); but almost all the early jurists understood the word to mean '*corruperit*' (spoil). And so Celsus asks, if you sow tares or wild oats in another man's crops and spoil them, not only can the owner bring the interdict against damage caused secretly or by force, but he can also proceed *in factum* under the Lex; and if a tenant-farmer proceeds thus he must give an undertaking that there will be no further legal proceedings – for example lest his landlord should seek to bring a further action. For it is one sort of damage to spoil or alter something so that the Lex Aquilia applies and quite another to add something that it is a nuisance to separate, but without any other change being made.

Celsus says that clearly the Aquilian action can be brought against someone who adulterates wine or pours it away or makes it sour or spoils it in any other way, because even pouring it away or making it sour are comprised within the term 'spoil'. And he does not deny that breaking and burning are included within the term 'spoiling' and says that there is nothing new in that a statute, after enumerating some cases specially, should add a general term which embraces those specific things; and this view is correct. We accept that 'to rend asunder' includes the case of him who wounds a slave either with a rod or whip or fist or strikes him with a weapon or in any other way that cuts him or makes a bruise, but only if wrongful damage is caused thereby. However, if he makes the slave in no way less valuable or less useful, the Aquilian action will not lie and the action for insult will have to be brought so far as this matter is concerned, for the Aquilian action avenges only those cases of breakage which cause loss. Therefore if a slave has not been rendered worse in point of his value, but expense is incurred in making him fit and healthy, it seems to me that in this respect loss has been caused, and accordingly it is possible to proceed under the Lex Aquilia.

If someone tears or stains clothes, he is liable under the Lex Aquilia as if he had broken something; and again, if someone pours my millet or corn into a river, the Aquilian action provides for this case. Again, if someone mixes up corn with sand or some other such thing so that separation is hard, it is possible to bring action as for a spoiling.

If a man knocks coins out of my hand, Sabinus thinks that there is an action for wrongful damage if they roll away and thus do not come into someone else's hands, if for example they fall into a river, or the sea, or into a drain. But if they

come into someone else's possession an action for aiding and
abetting theft may be brought – and the early jurists held this
view. Sabinus says that an *actio in factum* can also be given.

If a slave or a mare has a miscarriage because of a blow struck
by you, Brutus says that you are liable to an Aquilian action
just as in the case of a breaking, and Vivanus writes that there
is an Aquilian action, the same as for a breaking, if someone
deliberately sinks a merchant ship.

If someone harvests olives before their due season or cuts
down green corn or unripe grapes he is liable under the Lex
Aquilia; but if they are ripe for harvest, the Aquilian action
does not lie, as no wrongful harm has been done; rather, he
has made you a gift of the costs involved in harvesting a crop
of this nature. But if he makes off with the crop after collecting it, he is liable for theft, unless, Octavenus adds in the case
of the grapes, he threw them down on the ground so that they
were a dead loss. He says the same about trees that can be cut:
if they are not yet ready, he who cuts them is liable under the
Lex; but if he cuts ripe wood, he will be liable for theft and
for cutting timber furtively. But if you thin a willow thicket
so as not to harm the trunks, you will not be liable under the
Lex Aquilia.

Further, if someone castrates your slave boy and thus
increases his value, Vivanus writes that the Lex Aquilia
should not apply, but that you should instead bring the action
for insult or sue under the edict of the Aediles for four times
his value.

If you hand over a cup for filigree work to be done, the
jeweller will be held liable if he breaks it through lack of skill,
but if it breaks not through his lack of expertise but because
it has weakening cracks he can be exonerated; and accordingly
craftsmen usually contract when things of this sort are entrusted
to them that the work shall not be done at their risk and this

provision excludes their liabilitiy both under the contract for their professional services and under the Lex Aquilia.

When a husband has given his wife some pearls and she pierces them so that they can be worn as a necklace, either against the will of her husband or without his knowledge, she is liable under the Lex Aquilia whether she is divorced or still married.

If someone breaks down or staves in the doors of my house or smashes down the house itself, he is liable under the Lex Aquilia; or if he wrecks my aqueduct, even though the materials which are smashed down are mine, nevertheless because it is not my land over which I bring the water, it is better to say that an *actio utilis* should be given.

If a stone falls out of a cart and ruins or smashes something, it is agreed that the carter is liable to the Aquilian action if he loaded the stones badly and it is for this reason that they fell.

If a man entrusts a hired slave with the driving of his mule and the slave ties it by the halter to his thumb but the mule tears itself away wrenching off his thumb and falls headlong, Mela writes that if the slave was inexperienced but was hired out as an expert, an action can be brought against the slave's owner on the contract of hire for damaging or disabling the mule; but if the mule was upset by someone hitting or scaring it, then the owner (that is the mule's owner as well as the slave's owner) will have an action under the Lex Aquilia against him who frightened it. However, it seems to me that on the same facts that found an action on the contract, an action under the Lex Aquilia also lies.

Again, if you hire someone to mend a vat full of wine and he punctures it so that all the wine runs out, Labeo maintains that an *actio in factum* must be brought.

28. (PAUL) People who dig pits to catch bears and deer are liable under the Lex Aquilia if they dig such pits in a public

place and something falls in and is damaged, but there is no such liability for pits made elsewhere, where it is usual to make them. But this action is only given for good reason, that is if no warning was given and the plaintiff did not know of the danger, nor could he have foreseen it; and many cases of this sort can be seen in which the plaintiff fails, because he could have avoided the danger;

29. (ULPIAN) as for example if you set traps in a place where you had no right to put them and your neighbour's cattle fall into them. If you cut back my projecting roof which I had no right to have above your house, Proculus writes that I can proceed against you for wrongful damage, for you should have brought an action against me to establish that I had no right to a projecting roof, nor is it just that I should suffer damage from your cutting back my beams. There is a decision otherwise in a rescript of the Emperor Severus, who laid down that a person through whose house a water pipe had been laid (other than in accordance with an easement⁵) could in his own right smash it up; and very properly, for the difference is that the former made the projection on his own land, whereas the latter acted on another's.

If your boat causes me damage through colliding with my skiff, it is a question which action is open to me. Proculus says that if it was in the power of the sailors to prevent the collision and it happened through their fault, an action under the Lex Aquilia can be brought against them, because it matters little whether you do damage by letting your boat run loose, or by bad steering or even with your own hand, because in all these ways I suffer damage caused by you; but if a rope broke or the vessel ran into mine when no one was in control of it, no action can be brought against the owner. Furthermore, Labeo writes that when a ship was blown by the force of the wind into the anchor ropes of another vessel, and the sailors cut the ropes, no action should be allowed if the vessel could be extricated in no other way than by severing the ropes. And both Labeo and Proculus thought the same about fishermen's nets in which a fishing boat got caught; but clearly if this was caused through the fault of the sailors, action could be brought under the Lex Aquilia. But where action is brought for wrongful damage *to* the nets no account is to be taken of the fish which were not caught because of the damage, as it is so uncertain whether they would have been caught. The same is true in the cases of the prospective catches of both hunters and bird-catchers.

If a ship sinks another vessel coming towards it, Alfenus says that an action for wrongful damage lies either against the helmsman or against the captain; but if the ship was subject to such forces that it could not be managed, no action should be given against the owner. However, if the collision was caused by fault on the part of the sailors, I think that affords a basis for the Aquilian action.

If a man cuts a ship's mooring rope an action *in factum* can be brought in respect of the ship which is lost in consequence.

One can sue by the action under this chapter of the Lex Aquilia for damage to all animals which are not classed as cattle, for example, damage to dogs; and the same may be said of boars and lions and all other wild beasts and birds.

Municipal magistrates may also be liable under the Lex Aquilia if they do any damage unlawfully. So if one of them seizes your cattle by way of security and kills them by starvation because he would not allow you to take them food, you must be allowed an *actio in factum*. Again if he thinks he is taking security under the provisions of a statute but he does not take it in accordance with the law and he returns your things worn and spoiled, it is said that the Lex Aquilia applies. And indeed the same must be said even if he did make the seizure properly under the statute; but on the other hand if a magistrate does some injury by violence against someone who resists lawful process he will not be liable under the Lex Aquilia, for even when a slave taken in execution has hanged himself no action lies.

It is settled that the words 'whatever was the value in the last thirty days', even though they do not include 'highest', must be accepted in that sense.

30. (PAUL) A man who kills another's slave caught in the act of adultery will not be liable under this Lex.

If a slave given as a pledge is killed, the action is available to the debtor. But it is asked whether an *actio utilis* should be given to the creditor because he may have an interest either because the debtor is not solvent or because he has lost his own right of action through lapse of time. But it is unjust that the defendant should be liable to both owner and creditor – unless one might think that the debtor should suffer no injustice in this case for he is benefited by the amount of his debt and whatever is recovered in excess of the debt can be recovered from the defendant; or perhaps from the start action should be allowed to the debtor for the excess of the damages over the debt.

And so in these cases in which an action is given to the creditor because of the poverty of his debtor or because he has lost his right of action, the creditor will have the action under the Lex Aquilia up to the amount of the debt, so that this benefits the debtor, but the Aquilian action is open to the debtor in respect of any amount exceeding the debt.

If someone consumes another's wine or corn this does not seem to be unlawful damage, and so an *actio utilis* should be given.

In the action which arises under this title both intentional and negligent wrongdoing is punished; and so, if a man sets fire to stubble or thorns in order to burn them up and the fire escapes further afield and spreads and burns another's crops or vineyard, we shall ask whether this occurred through his inexperience or negligence. If he did it on a windy day, he is guilty of a mischief (for even he who provides the opportunity is deemed to have done the harm); and he who did not see to it that the fire did not spread stands in the same position. But if he saw to everything that he should have done, or it was a sudden squall of wind that extended the fire, he is free of fault.

If a slave is wounded, but not mortally, and he dies of neglect, the action will be for wounding, not for killing.

31. (PAUL) If a pruner threw down a branch from a tree and killed a slave passing underneath (the same applies to a man working on a scaffold), he is liable only if it falls down in a public place and he failed to shout a warning so that the accident could be avoided. But Mucius says that even if the accident occurred in a private place an action can be brought if his conduct is blameworthy – and he thinks there is fault when what could have been foreseen by a diligent man was not foreseen, or when a warning was shouted too late for the danger to be avoided. Following the same reasoning it does not matter much whether the deceased was making his way through a public or a private place, as the general public often make their way across private places. But if there is no path, the defendant should be liable only for positive wrongdoing, so he should not throw anything at someone he sees passing by; but on the other hand he is not to be deemed blameworthy when he could not have guessed that someone was about to pass through that place.

32. (GAIUS) It has been asked whether the practice of the proconsul in cases of theft by a gang of slaves (that is that the demand of the penalty should not be allowed against each one individually, but it suffices if payment is made of what would have been due had one free man done the theft) should be followed also in an action for unlawful damage. But it has seemed best that the same rule should be observed, and rightly too; for the reasoning in the action for theft is that the owner

of the slaves should not lose his whole household because of one delict; and the same reasoning being similarly applied to a case of wrongful damage, it follows that the same assessment of damages should be made especially as this form of delict is often less serious, as for instance when damage is done by negligence and not by malice.

If the same person wounds and then afterwards kills the same slave, he will be held liable for both a wounding and a killing, for there are two delicts. It is otherwise when one kills by many blows delivered in the same attack; for then there will be but one action for killing.

33. (PAUL) If you kill my slave, I think that personal feelings should not be taken into account (as where someone kills your natural son whom you would be prepared to buy for a great price) but only what he would be worth to the world at large. Sextius Pedius says that the prices of things are to be taken generally and not according to personal affections nor their special utility to particular individuals; and accordingly he says that he who has a natural son is none the richer because he would redeem him for a great price if someone else possessed him, nor does he who possesses someone else's son actually have as much as he could sell him for to his father. For under the Lex Aquilia we sue for the amount of the harm suffered and we are said to have lost either whatever we could have gained or what we are obliged to pay out.

In cases of damage not covered by the Lex Aquilia an *actio in factum* is given.

34. (MARCELLUS) The slave Stichus was bequeathed to both Titius and Seius. While Seius was still making up his mind, when Titius had already renounced the legacy, Stichus was killed. Thereupon Seius vindicated the legacy. Then Titius can proceed as if he were the sole legatee,

35. (ULPIAN) because his ownership is deemed to have accrued to him retrospectively;

36. (MARCELLUS) for just as a legacy becomes the heir's when a legatee has renounced it, so does Titius have the action as if he were the sole legatee.

If the owner directs that a slave whom Titius has mortally injured should be freed and become his heir and later Maevius succeeds him, Maevius will not have an action against Titius under the Lex Aquilia, at least according to the opinion of Sabinus, who thought that no action could be transmitted to the heir which was not open to the deceased; and indeed it would turn out absurd if the heir could recover damages as a consequence of the killing of the person whom he succeeded as heir. But if the master had ordered the freed slave to be a part-heir, his co-heir could proceed under the Lex Aquilia on account of his death.

37. (JAVOLENUS) If a free man acting under orders causes damage by his own hand, the action under the Lex Aquilia lies against the person who gave the orders, provided he had a right to give them; but if he had no such right, the action must be brought against the actual wrongdoer.

If a quadruped, on account of which a *pauperies*[6] action is being brought against its owner, is killed by someone else and an Aquilian action is brought against the killer, the damages must be assessed not according to the beast's physical value, but in the light of liability in the case involving the *pauperies* action, and accordingly he who killed it must be condemned in the Aquilian action to pay the amount that it would have profited the owner to make a noxal surrender rather than pay the damages as assessed.

38. (JAVOLENUS) It is generally agreed that I have a good case against you under the Lex Aquilia if my slave, whom you had bought in good faith, was wounded by one of your own slaves while he was in your service.

39. (POMPONIUS) Quintus Mucius writes as follows: a mare was grazing in someone else's meadow and when she was

driven out, she miscarried, as she was pregnant. It was asked whether or not her owner could sue, under the Lex Aquilia, the person who drove her off, because in striking her he had done her an injury. It was thought that the owner could bring action if he had struck her too hard or purposely driven her too violently.

Pomponius says that even though a person finds someone else's cattle on his land, he should show the same care in driving them off as if those he had found were his own, for if he has suffered any harm on their account he has his own legal remedies. And therefore he who finds someone else's cattle in his field may not lawfully impound them nor must he drive them out other than as we have just said above, that is, as though they were his own; but he must either remove them without hurting them or tell their owner, so that he can come and collect them.

40. (PAUL) If I allege that my handwritten receipt has been erased when it had been recorded that I was owed a sum of money subject to a condition, and for the present I am able to prove this by witnesses (who may not be available when the condition is fulfilled), I ought to win the case under the Lex Aquilia if I can briefly lead evidence to get the judge to accept the likely truth of my tale; but then it is open to me to enforce the judgement only after the condition attached to the debt has been fulfilled; so if it fails, the judgement will have no force.

41. (ULPIAN) Let us see whether an action lies for wilful damage if a man destroys a will. Marcellus, doubting this in the fifth book of his *Digest*, says that such action does not lie; for how, he says, can the damage be assessed? I made a note in his book that this is certainly true from the testator's point of view, for his interest cannot be valued, but that it is otherwise for an heir or a legatee, for to them wills are almost like signed receipts, and in the very same book Marcellus writes

that when a receipt is erased, action lies under the Lex Aquilia.

And if someone who is looking after someone's will makes an erasure, or reads it out with other people present, it is better to bring an action *in factum*, or sue for *iniuria* if he published the secrets of one's legal affairs with an insulting intent. Pomponius most elegantly says that sometimes it happens that a man does not render himself liable for theft by destroying a document, but he does incur liability for wrongful damage, as for instance where he does it with that intent. He will not then be liable for theft, because theft requires the deed to be accompanied by theftuous intent.

42. (JULIAN) Anyone who is looking after a will or a title deed and alters it so that it cannot be read is liable to an action on the contract of deposit and also to an action for its production in court because he has returned and produced the thing in a damaged state. The Aquilian action also lies on these same facts, for it is rightly said that he who has falsified a document has spoiled it.

43. (POMPONIUS) You have an action under the Lex Aquilia on account of damage done to property comprised in your inheritance before you took it up but after the death of the person whose heir you are, for the Lex Aquilia does not regard as 'owner' only him who was owner at the time the damage was done. If that were so, right of action could not pass from an ancestor to his heir, nor could you sue on your return home on account of what was done to your property while you were a prisoner of war. The law could not be otherwise without great unfairness to posthumous children who are heirs to their fathers.

We shall also say the same about trees cut down secretly during the same period. I think also that the same can be said about the special action for damage inflicted by force or in secret which lies if a person causes damage after express prohibition or if it becomes clear that he ought to have known that he would have been warned off by those to whom the inheritance belonged.

44. (ULPIAN) Under the Lex Aquilia even the slightest degree of fault counts. Whenever a slave does a wounding or killing with his master's knowledge, the master is without doubt liable to the Aquilian action.

45. (PAUL) We accept knowledge here as including sufferance, so that he who could have prevented harm is liable for not doing so.

One can proceed under the Lex Aquilia even if a wounded slave recovers.

If you kill my slave, believing that he is a free man, you will be liable under the Lex Aquilia.

When two slaves were jumping over some burning straw they bumped into each other, fell, and one was burnt to death. No action can be brought on that account if it is not known which was knocked over by which.

Those who do damage because they cannot otherwise defend themselves are blameless; for all laws and all legal systems allow one to use force to defend oneself against violence. But if in order to defend myself I throw a stone at my attacker and I hit not him but a passer-by, I shall be liable under the Lex Aquilia, for it is permitted only to use force against an attacker and even then only so far as is necessary for self-defence and not for revenge.

46. (ULPIAN) If action has been brought under the Lex Aquilia when a slave has been wounded one can none the less bring another action under the Lex if he later dies of the wound,

47. (JULIAN) but if after damages have been assessed in the first action and then when the slave has died his owner starts proceedings for the killing he will be prevented by the plea of fraud from recovering more in the two actions than he would have won by bringing an action for the killing in the first place.

48. (PAUL) If a slave damages property in an inheritance before the heir takes it up and then does other damage to that same property after he has been freed, he will be liable to both actions because these actions arise from separate causes.

49. If someone drives away, or even kills, another's bees by making smoke, he seems rather to have provided the cause of their death than directly to have killed them, and so he will be liable to an action *in factum*.

What is said about suing under the Lex Aquilia for damage done wrongfully must be taken as meaning that damage is done wrongfully when it inflicts wrong together with the damage, and this is inflicted, save where it is done under compulsion of overwhelming necessity, as Celsus writes about the man who pulled down his neighbour's house to keep a fire off his own; for he writes here that there is no action under the Lex Aquilia because he pulled down the adjoining house in the reasonable fear that the fire would reach his own house. Celsus also thinks that there is no action under the Lex, regardless of whether the fire would actually have reached him or been put out first.

50. (ULPIAN) But he who pulls down someone else's house against the owner's will and puts up baths on the site is liable to an action for the damage caused, quite apart from the rule of natural law that whatever is built on land belongs to the owner of the land.

51. (JULIAN) A slave who had been wounded so gravely that he was certain to die of the injury was appointed someone's heir and subsequently killed by a further blow from another assailant. The question is whether action under the Lex Aquilia lies against both assailants for killing him. The answer was given as follows: a person is generally said to have killed if he furnished a cause of death in any way whatever, but so far as the Lex Aquilia is concerned, there will be liability only if the death resulted from some application of force, done as it

were by one's own hand, for the law depends on the interpretation of the Latin word *caedere*. Furthermore, it is not only those who wound so as to deprive at once of life who will be liable for a killing in accordance with the Lex, but also those who inflict an injury that is certain to prove fatal. Accordingly, if someone wounds a slave mortally and then after a while someone else inflicts a further injury, as a result of which he dies sooner than would otherwise have been the case, it is clear that both assailants are liable for killing. This rule has the authority of the ancient jurists, who decided that if a slave were injured by several persons but it was not clear which blow actually killed him, they would all be liable under the Lex Aquilia. But in the case that we are considering the dead slave will not be valued in the same way in assessing the penalty to be paid for each wound. The person who struck him first will have to pay the highest value of the slave in the preceding year, counting back three hundred and sixty-five days from the day of the wounding; but the second assailant will be liable to pay the highest price that the slave would have fetched had he been sold during the year before he departed this life – and of course in this figure the value of the inheritance will be included. Therefore, for the killing of this slave, one assailant will pay more and the other less, but this is not to be wondered at because each is deemed to have killed him in different circumstances and at a different time. But in case anyone might think that we have reached an absurd conclusion, let him ponder carefully how much more absurd it would be to hold that neither should be liable under the Lex Aquilia, or that one should be held to blame rather than the other. Misdeeds should not escape unpunished and it is not easy to decide if one is more blameworthy than the other. Indeed, it can be proved by innumerable examples that the civil law has accepted things for the general good that do not accord with pure logic. Let us content ourselves for the time being with just one instance: when several people, with intent to steal, carry off a beam which no single one of them could have carried alone, they are all liable to an action for theft, although by subtle reasoning one could make the point that no single one of them could be liable because in literal truth he could not have moved it unaided.

52. (ALFENUS) If a slave were to die as the result of an assault, and without any contributory factor like neglect on the part of his owner or lack of professional skill in a doctor, an action may properly be brought for killing him wrongfully.

One night a shopkeeper had placed a lantern above his display counter which adjoined the footpath, but some passer-by took it down and carried it off. The shopkeeper pursued him, calling for his lantern, and caught hold of him; but in order to escape from his grasp the thief began to hit the shop-keeper with the whip that he was carrying, on which there was a spike. From this encounter a real brawl developed in which the shopkeeper put out the eye of the lantern-stealer and he asked my opinion as to whether he had inflicted wrongful damage, bearing in mind that he had been hit with the whip first. My opinion was that unless he had poked out the eye intentionally he would not appear to have incurred liability, as the damage was really the lantern-stealer's own fault for hitting him first with the whip; on the other hand, if he had not been provoked by the beating, but had started the brawl when trying to snatch back his lantern, the shop-keeper would appear to be accountable for the loss of the eye.

Some mules were pulling two loaded carts up the Capitol Hill. The front cart had tipped up, so the drivers were trying to lift the back to make it easier for the mules to pull it up the hill, but suddenly it started to roll backwards. The muleteers, seeing that they would be caught between the two carts, leapt out of its path and it rolled back and struck the rear cart, which careered down the hill and ran over someone's slave boy. The owner of the boy asked me whom he should sue. I replied that it all depended on the facts of the case. If the drivers who were holding up the front cart had got out of its way of their own accord and that had been the reason why the mules could not take the weight of the cart and had been pulled back by it, in my opinion no action could be brought against the owner of the mules. The boy's owner should rather sue the men who had been holding up the cart; for damage is no less wrongful when someone voluntarily lets go of something in such circumstances and it hits someone else. For example, if a man failed to restrain an ass that he was driving he would be liable for any damage that he caused, just as if he threw a missile or anything else from his hand. But if the accident that we are considering had occurred because the mules had shied at something and the drivers had left the cart for fear of being crushed, no action would lie against them; but in such a case action should be brought against the owner of the mules. On the other hand, if neither the mules nor the drivers were at fault, as for example if the mules just could not take the weight, or if in trying to do so they had slipped and fallen and the cart had then rolled down the hill because the men could not hold it when it tipped up, there would be no liability on the owner or on the drivers. It is quite clear, furthermore, that however the accident happened, no action could be brought against the owner of the mules pulling the cart behind, for they fell back down the hill not through any fault of theirs, but because they were struck by the cart in front.

A man sold some oxen on approval, but while they were on trial one of them gored the buyer's slave. My opinion was taken as to the seller's liability for the damage. I said that if the oxen had already been bought he would not be liable, but if they were still on approval he would be, if the goring had happened because the ox was vicious – though he would not be responsible if it had been the slave's own fault.

Take this case of some people playing ball. One of them pushed a little slave boy when he was trying to pick up the ball and he fell and broke his leg. When I was asked if I thought his owner could sue the person who had pushed him over, I replied that he could not, as it seemed to me to be a purely accidental injury.

53. (NERATIUS) You have driven someone else's oxen into a narrow place and the result was that they fell over a precipice. An *actio in factum* based on the Lex Aquilia will be given against you.

54. (PAPINIAN) An action under the Lex Aquilia is available to a debtor when a person to whom an animal has been contractually promised wounds that animal before the time of performing the contract has passed; and the same is true if he kills the animal. But if the promisee kills it when the promisor is in default on his promise, even though the debtor may be released, this is not an occasion when the Lex Aquilia can properly be brought into operation, for the creditor is deemed to have done an injury to himself rather than to anyone else.

55. (PAUL) I promised to Titius either one of two slaves, Stichus or Pamphilus – Stichus being worth 10,000 and Pamphilus 20,000.[7] Titius killed Stichus before I was in default. A question was then put about an action under the Lex Aquilia. I answered: since it is put that he has killed the cheaper of the two, for the purposes of this case the creditor is in no different position from any third party. What then should the measure of damages be: 10,000, that is, the value of the dead Stichus, or the value of the one I should now hand over? In other words, what is the value of my interest? What should we say if Pamphilus also dies, without any default on my part? Will the value of Stichus be less because the promisor is released from his obligation? It is enough to say that he was worth more when he was killed or within a year. On this principle, even if he were killed within a year of the death of

Pamphilus he will be deemed to have been worth the greater value.

56. (PAUL) If a wife causes damage to her husband's property she can be sued under the Lex Aquilia.

57. (JAVOLENUS) I lent you a horse and when you were out on it in the company of a number of riders, one of them bumped into you and threw you off, and in the accident the horse's legs were broken. In such a case, Labeo would have it that there is no action against you but that if it happened because of a rider's negligence there would be a right of action against that rider. He says it is clear that no action lies against the owner of the horse, and I agree.

CONCERNING THEFT

◇

1. (PAUL) Labeo says that the very word for theft (*furtum*) is itself derived from a Latin word meaning 'black', because it is committed secretly, in the dark and most often in the night; or it may be derived from a corruption of a word for fraud (*fraus*), as Sabinus said; or from the similar Latin words 'to carry' (*ferre*) and 'to carry away' (*auferre*); or it may come from the Greek language in which a thief is denoted by a similar-sounding word – and the Greeks themselves derive their own word for a thief (φώρ) from the verb 'to carry' (φέρειν). Thus it is that the mere intention to steal does not make a man a thief, and accordingly a man who has received someone else's property for safekeeping and then denies his obligation is not liable to an action for theft without more ado, though he is so liable if he conceals that property in order to appropriate it for himself.

Theft is a dishonest handling of a thing in order to gain by it or by its use or possession. Such conduct is against the very law of nature.

2. (GAIUS) There are two degrees of theft: manifest and non-manifest.

3. (ULPIAN) A manifest thief is one whom the Greeks describe as 'caught in the very act', that is, one who is caught with the stolen goods on him. It matters little who it is who actually catches him – whether it is the owner of the stolen goods, or anyone else. But it may be asked whether a thief is

only a manifest thief if he is caught in the very act of stealing or indeed whether it is good enough that he be apprehended just anywhere. The better view – and this was Julian's opinion – is that even if he is not caught in the place where he committed the theft, he is nevertheless a manifest thief if he is caught with the stolen thing on him before he has taken it to the place he intended.

4. (PAUL) 'The place he intended to carry it to' is understood as 'the place where he intended to stop that day with the stolen thing'.

5. (ULPIAN) Therefore irrespective of whether he is caught in a public or in a private place, so long as he has not yet borne the thing to the place he was making for, the charge will be one of manifest theft if he is caught with the stolen thing on him: and that was the view of Cassius. But if he has got his loot home, even if he is caught with the stolen things in his possession, he is not a manifest thief.

6. (PAUL) For although theft may be committed many times over by successive handlings of the stolen goods, it was thought right to determine whether or not a theft was manifest at the time of the original thieving.

7. (ULPIAN) Let us consider whether a man who committed theft while he was yet a slave, but was caught only after he had been freed from slavery, could be a manifest thief. Pomponius took the view that one could not proceed against him for manifest theft because the original theft, done while he was still a slave, was not manifest. In the same passage Pomponius remarks very neatly that a thief is only made manifest by the manner of his arrest; and further, if you saw me committing a theft in your house, but hid yourself for fear that I might kill you, even though you watched me, it is not a case of manifest theft. But Celsus extends the meaning of catching like this: if you see the thief carrying something off and run to arrest him, but he makes his escape by throwing away his

loot, that is manifest theft; and in his view it matters little whether the owner of the goods makes the arrest or a neighbour, or any passer-by.

8. (GAIUS) What sort of theft is non-manifest is clear: for a stealing which is not within the meaning of manifest theft must be non-manifest theft.

9. (POMPONIUS) Once someone has a right to bring an action of theft, continued handling of the stolen thing by the thief will not give him any further right of action for theft even though there may have been an increase or growth of the stolen thing meanwhile. But even if I brought a *vindicatio* against the thief my right to recover by *condictio*[8] remains, though it can be said to be within the competence of the judge who hears the action on the proprietary issues to hold the two cases together so that he can make an order for restitution only if the plaintiff abandons the *condictio* action. However, if the defendant has already had judgement given against him in the *condictio* and paid the amount assessed, the judge should either dismiss the *vindicatio* or (as most people think) if the plaintiff is prepared to pay back that amount but the defendant refuses to give back the stolen slave, he should order him to pay the value as sworn under oath by the plaintiff.

10. (ULPIAN) Anyone whose interest it is that the property should not be stolen can bring an action for theft.

11. (PAUL) But he can only bring the action if his interest in the thing is an honest interest.

12. (ULPIAN) Thus a cleaner who has taken in clothes for cleaning or mending can bring an action if they are stolen from him, provided he is solvent, because he is responsible in his contract for their safekeeping. But if he is not solvent, the right to sue for theft passes to the owner of the clothes, for there can be nothing at risk for a man who already has nothing more to lose. But an action in theft is not available to one who possesses things in bad faith, even though it is in his interest

that they should not be stolen; for no one can acquire a right of action by his own dishonesty – and also the law gives such a right only to someone who possesses property in good faith.

In the case of goods pledged for security with a pawnbroker, we give the action for their theft to the pawnbroker even though the goods are no part of his own property; and indeed we allow him the right to sue not only a third party, but even the owner himself, as Julian wrote. But it is thought right to allow an action to the owner as well, and thus it may happen that the same person could be both plaintiff and defendant.

The action is thus available to both, because both have an interest in the safety of the goods. But is this always in the creditor's interest, or is it only in his interest when the pledgor is unable to redeem the pledge? Pomponius thought that the pawnbroker is always concerned to keep the pledge safely and Papinian agreed with this; and indeed it is the better view that the creditor seems always to have an interest. Julian said this many times.

13. (PAUL) He to whom something is owed under a contract of stipulation does not have an action in theft if that thing is stolen so that the debtor cannot hand it over, even though he be in default.

14. (ULPIAN) Celsus wrote that a purchaser has no action in theft if the thing sold to him is not handed over; but as yet the vendor has the right of action, though clearly he can be made to assign to the buyer not only the action in theft, but also the *condictio* and the *vindicatio* as well; and he must also make over whatever he has recovered through these actions. This is undoubtedly good law, and Julian agrees. It is certainly the case that the goods are at the purchaser's risk, so long as the vendor takes proper care of them until delivery, but so clearly is it the law that the buyer has no right of action for theft of the goods before delivery that it has been queried whether the purchaser himself would be liable in theft if he were to steal

the thing. Julian says this in the twenty-third volume of his *Digest*: if the purchaser having paid the price carries off the thing for the safety of which the seller is responsible, he is not liable to an action for theft; but clearly, if he takes the thing before paying the price, he is liable, just as if he had wrongly taken away property which he had pawned. Furthermore, tenants have the right of action for theft, even though they are not owners of the tenants' property, because they have the necessary interest in it.

Let us see whether a depositee can bring an action for theft: since he is only liable for fraudulent misuse, the law very properly does not afford him an action for theft, for what is his interest provided he keeps clear of fraud? And even if he is guilty of fraudulently misusing it, the risk of the property is still his, for he should not be able to sue in an action of theft as a result of his own fraud. Julian indeed wrote as follows in the twenty-second volume of his *Digest*: just as it is agreed law as regards thieves in general that they cannot bring an action in theft in respect of a thing which they themselves stole, similarly a depositee cannot sue for theft even though the risk of the property was his at the time when it was meddled with.

Papinian ponders the following case: if I accept two slaves as security for a debt of 10 *aurei* and one is stolen, but the other one who remains is alone worth not less than 10 *aurei*, whether I have an action in theft for only 5 *aurei*, because the one I still have is good for the other 5; or is it right that because the one I have might die, I should claim 10 in my action, even though the slave I still hold is of sufficient value? This last was Papinian's view. He says that we should consider not so much the value of the security which the thief did not take, but rather that which he did. Considering another problem, he writes that if, when 10 are owed to me and a slave given in security for that amount is stolen, I recover 10 by an action for theft and then the slave is stolen again, I cannot bring action a second time, for my interest in that slave has lapsed when I have recovered the amount owed to me once. All this is true only if he is stolen without fault on my part; for if there is fault on my part I then have a valuable interest, because I would be liable in an action for recovery of the pledge. But if I am not at fault there is no doubt that the action not available to the creditor is open to the owner of the slave; and Pomponius also holds this view in his tenth book on Sabinus. These authorities also say that if the two slaves are stolen at the same time the pledgee may bring action in respect of each one, not for the full amount for each slave but for such part of the whole debt as each of them is worth to him. But if the two slaves are stolen at separate times, if the creditor recovers his whole debt in respect of one, the other will not be worth anything to him. Again Pomponius writes that if someone to whom I lend something is guilty of fraud in respect of the borrowed property I cannot sue him in theft; and he takes the same view of someone who has accepted a commission to convey property.

It is queried whether a father has an action of theft in respect of property lent to his son. Julian thinks that a father cannot proceed in this case because he is not liable for its safekeeping. He says this is just like the situation of someone who has guaranteed a borrower, and he cannot bring the action either, for he says that it is not everyone who is interested in the safety of the thing who can bring an action of theft, but only he who would be held liable if the thing should be lost by his default. Celsus states this view in the twelfth volume of the *Digest*. If a slave who had been lent gratuitously is stolen, one may ask whether the borrower has a right of action for theft; and seeing he is not himself liable for an action arising from the borrowing (because this sort of arrangement is akin to a free gift – indeed it is for this reason that the interdict was made available) he will not have an action. It is indeed true that after the interdict is issued he becomes liable for fault and therefore he can also at that time sue for theft. But if someone has hired something, he will have a right to sue for theft provided the stealing was through no fault of his.

If a son in power of his father is carried off it is obvious that the father has a right of action. If a thing is lent and the borrower of it dies before return, although there can be no theft of an inheritance, so that the heir cannot sue, the lender certainly can. And the same applies if the thing was pledged or hired; for although it be granted that no action lies in respect of a stolen inheritance, he in whose interest it is that the thing should not be stolen most certainly acquires a right to sue.

He who borrows something not only has a right to sue for the thing itself but also for anything that is produced from it, for he is just as responsible for this as he is for the thing itself. For example, if you borrow a slave you may sue if his clothes are stolen even though you did not specifically also borrow the clothes he was wearing. Similarly, if you borrow from me a team of horses and a foal goes along with them, I have no doubt that you may sue a thief of the foal even though it was not included in our agreement. And so it is asked: 'What sort of action of theft is it that the borrower has?' I think that actions of theft are available for all those who hold other people's goods at their own risk, as in cases of borrowing, hiring and pledging, if those things are stolen; but the *condictio* is available only to the owner.

If I send you a letter and it is stolen while in the post, who can bring action for the theft? First of all we must ask who the letter belongs to – to the sender or to him to whom it was addressed. If I hand it to the addressee's slave, it immediately becomes the addressee's property; or if I hand it to his agent, equally so, since property may be acquired also through a free man, it becomes the addressee's, and particularly if he had an interest in becoming owner. But if I sent the letter on the understanding that it would be returned to me, I continue to be the owner because I did not wish to lose or transfer ownership. Who then should bring the action for theft? It is he who had an interest in its not being stolen, that is, whoever stood to gain by whatever was written in it. Thus it can be asked whether the messenger who was given the letter to deliver can bring an action for theft. He can if he was responsible for its safekeeping and thus had an interest of his own in its delivery – for example the letter may have contained instructions to give the bearer something or do something for him. If so he can bring an action, as he also can if he undertook responsibility for its safety or was to be paid for delivering it. In such a case he will be in the same position as an innkeeper or the master of a ship; and we allow them the right of action, provided they are solvent, because they stand to bear the risk for loss of things entrusted to them.

15. (PAUL) The interest of a pawnbroker from whom a pledge is stolen is not just the amount of the debt, but he can bring action for the full value of the pledge, though in a pawnbroker's action he can be made to hand over to his debtor any amount recovered in excess of his due.

An owner who seizes his own property in which someone else has a usufruct is liable to an action for theft on the part of the usufructuary; but Pomponius writes that he who lends you something and then takes it back cannot be sued by you for theft because you have no interest since you are not yourself liable to be sued on that loan. However, if you have some right of retention because of expense incurred on the thing lent to you, you will have an action against the owner if he purloins it, because in such a case the thing is, as it were, a sort of security.

16. (PAUL) Nor can a father bring an action for theft against a son in his family, a restriction which is not because of any provision of the law, but which arises from the very nature of

the situation, for a man can no more sue a person subject to his *potestas* than he can sue himself.

17. (ULPIAN) Our slaves or sons *in potestate* who commit theft against us are not liable to an action of theft; for a man who can deal with a thief just as he pleases does not need to take him to court for theft. Accordingly no such action has been handed down to us by the ancient jurists. From this proposition there arises a question – if the slave is sold or manumitted will he be liable to an action for theft? – and it seems that he will not; for just as no action can be raised against him at the outset, none can arise afterwards. Clearly though, if he meddles further after his manumission, it must be said that he can be liable for theft, because a further theft is committed now.

When a slave which I have bought and had delivered to me is returned by me on rescission of the sale, the situation is not on that account just as if he had never been mine, but that he was mine and has ceased to be mine. Therefore, says Sabinus, if he committed theft, the purchaser who rescinded the sale cannot bring the action; and although he cannot sue, he can still nevertheless claim that compensation is owing to him for the misdeed committed before the rescission, and this will be taken into account in the action to rescind the sale.

This further question is asked: if a slave who was running away stole from his master could he bring an action against the bona fide possessor of the slave, before the slave has returned and come again into his power? The point is that although I am deemed to possess my slave even after he has run away, I am nevertheless not liable if he steals because he is not in my power – Julian says that the possession I am deemed to have is only of use to me for the bare legal purpose of acquiring him by length of time of possession. Accordingly Pomponius says in the sixteenth book of his writings on Sabinus that the owner of a runaway slave can bring the action.

18. (PAUL) When it is said that 'liability attaches to the guilty

party' that is true only to the extent that a right of noxal surrender arises against someone at the moment when the wrong is committed and attaches to the person of the wrongdoer until he gets into such a position that had he been so placed at the time of the offence, no such liability would have arisen. Thus, if your slave steals my property and I later become his owner and then sell him, Cassius and his school are of the opinion that I cannot sue the buyer.

19. (ULPIAN) In an action for theft it is enough if the thing stolen is described sufficiently for it to be identified. It is not necessary to speak of the weight of vessels, for example, and it is therefore enough to refer to 'a plate', 'a dish' or 'a cup' – but its material should be added, whether it be silver or gold or anything else. But if someone brings an action for unwrought silver, he should speak of a 'lump of silver' and give its weight. In the case of silver coins their number must be stated, and similarly how many gold coins have been taken by theft. It is debated whether the colour of a dress need be specified and indeed it is desirable that it should; for just as in the case of a gold cup the material is stated, so in the case of a dress the colour should be given, though clearly if a man swears on oath that he cannot say for certain what the colour is he must be relieved of this particular obligation.

Anyone who pawns a thing and then purloins it is liable to an action for theft. The owner of a pledged object is deemed to commit theft not only when he carries it off from his creditor who has it in his possession, or indeed in his hands, but even if he takes it when it is not in the creditor's possession, as for example if the owner sells it after pledging it. It is settled that in such a case he is also guilty of theft, and that was Julian's opinion also.

20. (PAUL) If a copper object is given as a pledge and the pledgor says it is gold, he is certainly acting disgracefully, but

he is not committing theft. But if having handed over something made of gold, he got it back by saying that he wanted to weigh it or add his seal and then substituted something of bronze base metal in its place, he commits theft, for he is meddling with the thing already pledged.

If you buy something from me, in good faith, and I carry it off, or if indeed you have a usufruct of something of mine and I interfere with it dishonestly, I shall be liable in your action for theft, even though I am the owner of that thing. But in these cases *usucapio* (acquisition through long possession) is not impeded as in the usual case of stolen things, for even if a third party had stolen it and then it came back into my hands, it could be usucaped.

21. (PAUL) It is a common question whether if someone takes a bushel out of a whole heap of corn, he commits theft of the heap or only of as much as he carried off. Ofilius says that he steals the whole heap. Consider the case of touching someone's ear. Trebatius says this seems to be a case of touching the whole person. Thence it follows that he who opens a cask and draws off a small quantity of wine seems to be a thief not only of what he takes but of the whole cask, though he will only be liable to pay damages for the amount he actually took. Take the case of a man who opens a chest which is too heavy to lift and handles everything inside and then goes away, but later comes back and carries off some item or other and is caught before reaching the place he was making for: in such a case he is both an 'ordinary thief' and a red-handed (manifest) thief in respect of the same thing. And similarly a man who cuts corn and handles it during daylight is both an ordinary thief and also a red-handed thief in respect of that which he is caught carrying off during the following night.

If a man who deposits a bag of twenty coins with someone else for safekeeping is later given back another bag of thirty (because of the other person's mistake) and thinks that his own twenty are among them, it seems that he is liable for theft as to the ten.

If someone steals some copper, thinking it is gold (or vice versa according to the eighth volume of Pomponius on Sabinus), or he thinks he takes a small amount of something whereas it is in fact a lot, he commits theft of that which he actually takes. Ulpian says the same. But if a thief takes two purses, one containing ten coins and the other twenty, of which he thinks one is his own and knows the other is someone else's, we will surely say he commits theft of only one, that is the one he knows is not his, just as if he took two cups, thinking one was his own and knowing that one was not – this also is theft of one only. But if he thought the handle of the cup was his – or indeed if it really was – this is still theft of the whole cup, according to Pomponius.

Again, if someone steals a bushel of corn from a whole shipload, is this theft of the whole cargo or just of the bushel? The problem can be considered more easily in respect of a full warehouse. Surely it is a bit hard to hold that this would be theft of the whole contents? But what then should be said of a cistern of wine, or of water – or what indeed of a ship carrying wine (and there are many ships whose holds are brimming with wine)? What shall we say of someone who draws off some of the wine? Would this be theft of the whole cargo? It is most likely that we would not go that far. There is no doubt though, if you put the case of jars in a storeroom and they are stolen, that that is not one theft of the whole store but of the individual jars, just as when a thief takes away one individual thing from among a number of movable things in a warehouse.

If someone enters a room with intent to steal he is not yet a thief, even though he entered in order to steal. Well then, to what action is he liable? Certainly he is liable to an action for *iniuria* (insult), or if he entered by force, he is liable to proceedings for violence.

Suppose someone opens or breaks into something too heavy to be moved. He is not liable to an action of theft for the whole thing but only for those things which he actually stole, because he cannot take the whole. Similarly if anyone opens a case of things which he cannot carry away in order to meddle with the contents and he does meddle with them, then even though he could manage to take away several of the individual things, he is only a thief of the particular things he takes and not of the whole if he cannot carry away the whole lot, case and all. However, if he was capable of carrying away the whole container we say that he is a thief of the whole lot, whether or not he opened it to take away the contents, or some of them, one at a time – and Sabinus says that this is so.

If two or more men steal a piece of timber which no one of them could lift by himself, it must be said that they are all equally liable for the whole theft even though no one of them could handle or remove it alone, and this is indeed the law, for we cannot say that each one committed a part of the theft, but the whole thing was the act of them all and thus each man is individually liable for the theft. But although a man may be guilty of the theft of things which he did not himself carry away he will not be liable to make restitution, because the relevant action only lies for the things which a man has actually taken – and thus Pomponius writes.

22. (PAUL) If a thief has smashed or broken something with which he was not meddling in order to steal, no action for theft lies against him in respect of that thing. By this reasoning, if a chest is broken open, so that pearls, say, may be taken away, and these are handled with intent to steal them, it seems that

theft is committed only as to the pearls; and this is right, for other things which are moved aside to get at the pearls are not handled with a view to theft of them.

A person who takes a scraping from a metal dish is a thief of the whole dish and is liable in an action of theft to the extent of its value to the owner.

23. (ULPIAN) Julian writes in his twenty-second book that a child can commit theft if he is old enough to be capable of dishonest intent; and moreover since a child can commit theft he can also be liable for unlawful damage too; but, he says, some limit must be set, so this rule does not apply to infants. I think that if a child is old enough to be legally blame-worthy he can be sued under the Lex Aquilia. It is also correct, as Labeo says, that a child cannot be liable as an accomplice in theft.

24. (PAUL) He is however liable to an action for the recovery of the stolen goods, as Julian writes.

25. (ULPIAN) What most of the authorities say – that there can be no action for theft of land – is correct. Therefore it is asked whether a man who has been turned off his land can bring an action for its recovery against the dispossessor. Labeo says not; but Celsus thinks he can bring a *condictio* for pos-session of land, just as he can when a movable thing is stolen. In the case of things carried off from land, like trees, stone, sand or crops which are gathered with intent to steal, there is no doubt that the action of theft can be brought.

26. (PAUL) If wild bees make a honeycomb in a tree on your land and someone carries off the bees or their honeycomb, you cannot sue him for theft, because they were never yours. It is settled that they are among the things acquired by their captors – on land, at sea or in the air. But it is also settled that a tenant-farmer may sue in theft anyone who carries off his standing crops because they become his property as soon as they are severed.

27. (ULPIAN) Anyone who steals the deeds or notes of a contract is liable to an action of theft not only for the value of the deeds themselves but also for what they were worth to the plaintiff.

28. (PAUL) But if the document is stolen first and obliterated later, the taker is liable for the value of the owner's interest in its not being taken: the obliteration will not increase the penalty.

29. (ULPIAN) An action can also be brought for its production in court and there will also be an action under the interdict to decide who it belongs to,

30. (ULPIAN) at least, if the defaced documents were among the property left by a deceased person.

31. (ULPIAN) Further, if someone defaces a picture or a book he can be sued for unlawful damage for having destroyed it.

If someone steals or falsifies deeds relating to the formal business of a city council, Labeo says he is liable for theft; and he says the same of other official documents and partnership papers.

32. (PAUL) Some say that in an action for the theft of deeds, their valuation is what they are themselves worth, because if you can prove to the judge before whom the case of theft is heard how much the debt owed to you was, you can just as well prove that debt before the judge who hears the case for its recovery; but if indeed you cannot establish that in your action of theft, neither could you prove just what your interest is. However, it is possible for a plaintiff to bring such an action after he somehow recovered the deeds, and thus can prove what the value of his interest would have been if he had not recovered them.

How the plaintiff can establish the value of his interest is a much more important matter in a case under the Lex Aquilia; for if he can prove the amount by other evidence, he does not suffer (further) loss. But suppose perchance a man made a loan of money subject to a condition and at first he had plenty of witnesses whose evidence would prove the amount of the loan – may they not die while the condition is still unresolved? Or what about this – suppose I have sued for the money owed to me and because I did not have there in court the witnesses and signatories who remembered the deal I lost both the action and my money; now though, when I sue for theft, I can make use of their memory and their testimony to establish the truth that I did lend the money.

33. (ULPIAN) A tutor is charged with the administration of his pupils' property, but he is not granted any power to appropriate anything for himself; and therefore if he takes anything with dishonest intent, he commits theft and moreover ownership of the thing cannot be acquired by long possession. Although action can be brought against him to account for his tutorship, he can also be held liable for theft too. This rule is laid down in respect of tutors, but the same applies to curators of young persons under twenty-five and indeed to all other curators.

34. (PAUL) He who aids and abets a theft is never himself a manifest thief; and therefore it can happen that the helper is liable for 'ordinary' theft while the actual perpetrator, when caught, is liable as a manifest thief, albeit that they were both involved in the same theft.

35. (POMPONIUS) If someone undertakes to carry goods and he knows they are stolen, it is settled law that if he is caught, that is a red-handed theft, at least so far as he is concerned; but if he did not know, then neither of them is a red-handed thief – the carrier is not because he was not the thief; and the thief was not because he was not caught.

Suppose one of your two slaves has drawn some water belonging to someone else and carried it away, but that the second is caught still in the act of drawing more water. You will be held liable for 'ordinary' theft on account of the first, but for red-handed theft by the second.

36. (ULPIAN) A person who persuades a slave to run away is not a thief, nor does anyone who simply gives bad advice to someone else commit theft, any more than anyone who persuades another to throw himself off a cliff or to lay violent hands on himself. No action for theft lies for this sort of thing. But if one man persuades a slave to run away, so that his colleague may capture him, he who does the persuading will be liable for theft because theft was committed by his aid and advice. Pomponius writes more on this point – he says that he who did the persuading, although he would not at that time be liable for theft, does become liable as soon as the other party begins to appropriate the runaway, because this seems to be a proper case of a theft by his aid and advice.

Similarly, it seems right that anyone who helps another's son, slave or wife in committing theft should himself be liable for theft, even though such thieves are not themselves liable to a theft action. Again, Pomponius says, if a runaway slave takes goods with him he who advised him can also be sued on account of those goods too, because he gave advice to the handler himself. Sabinus says the same.

If two slaves encourage each other to run away and they both abscond together, neither of them can be a thief of the other.

What then if they both concealed each other – is it possible that they could then be thieves of each other? It can be said that each was a thief of the other to the extent that if other people stole them individually they would be liable if each gave counsel and advice to the other. By the same reasoning Sabinus says they would both be liable for any goods which the other took away with him.

37. (POMPONIUS) If my tame peacock strays from my house.

and you chase it until it dies, I can sue you in theft as soon as anyone takes possession of it.

38. (PAUL) A mother has no action in theft if her son is stolen from her. There can be an action in theft on account of a free person, but there is no *condictio* for them.

39. (ULPIAN) It is true that if someone carries off or conceals someone else's slave who is a prostitute, this is not necessarily theft; for we must consider not only the act, but also its motive – and if the motive was lust, this is not theft. Accordingly even he who broke down a prostitute's door to gratify his desires and thereby let in thieves (acting independently, not in concert with him) who carried off her property is not guilty of theft. But would a man be liable under the Lex Fabia[9] if he secretly harboured a harlot to satisfy his lusts? I do not think so, and I base this opinion on a case which actually happened. In this case he acts more basely than someone who steals, but this is balanced by the disgrace he brings on himself. At all events it is clear that he is not a thief.

40. (PAUL) A person who takes hired horses further than the contract stipulated, or uses someone else's property without his consent, commits theft.

41. (ULPIAN) If a theft is committed against a person's property while he is a prisoner of war and he returns with the benefit of *postliminium*,[10] we can say that he has an action of theft.

It is certain that an adopting parent can sue on account of a theft from the person he is adopting provided the theft occurred before the adoption was completed; if the theft was after the adoption, no possible doubt even arises.

As long as the thief lives, the right of action survives; for the thief must be either *sui iuris* and responsible for his own actions, or else he has come into someone else's *potestas* and there is then a right of action against that person to whose power he is subject. This is expressed in our maxim *noxa caput sequitur* (the guilt attaches to the offender). We should consider whether the right to sue is extinguished if a man is reduced into slavery by the enemy after he has committed a delict. Pomponius wrote that it was extinguished, but that if the offender returns the action revives, either by *postliminium* (our law's restoration of civil rights to captives when they return home), or in some other way, and that is the present law.

42. (PAUL) If a slave works his master's ship without permission and any goods are lost, an action with the usual formula is given against his master so that in respect of what anyone else lost it will refer to liability 'up to the amount of the slave's *peculium*'; whereas in respect of the slave's own fault it will provide in the alternative for his noxal surrender. Therefore, if the slave had been freed before action is brought, action up to the extent of his *peculium* will be available against his owner for a year, though the noxal liability still attaches to the slave personally. Sometimes both the freed slave and his manumittor remain liable for theft, if for example he freed him to try to avoid the liability; but Sabinus was of the opinion that if the action is brought against the owner, the manumitted slave is freed from the liability, just as if the case had actually been decided.

43. (ULPIAN) If a false creditor (that is, someone who dishonestly pretends that he is owed a debt) accepts money, he thereby commits theft and the coins do not become his; and a false agent seems to commit theft in the same way. But Neratius says this may seem to be so only subject to this distinction, namely that it is certainly correct when a debtor hands money to the supposed agent for him to pass it to the creditor and the agent embezzles it. In such a case the money continues to belong to the debtor because the supposed agent does not accept it on behalf of the person to whom the debtor intended it to pass, and thus without doubt commits theft by handling it against the will of the owner. But if the

debtor hands over the money intending to pass ownership of it to the agent, Neratius says that he can in no way commit theft of it because he receives it with the consent of the owner.

If a man receives money which is not owed to him and directs that payment should be made to someone else, that will not be a theft by him if he is not there when the payment is made; but it is otherwise if he is present, in which case he commits theft. If a man does not actually lie about his identity but uses words misleadingly, that is deceit rather than theft; for example, he may say that he is a rich man, or is going to spend what he receives in buying goods, or promises to find substantial sureties or undertakes to pay the money back very shortly. In such cases he is guilty of deception rather than theft, as he will not be liable in an action of theft. But he is fraudulent, so if there is no other action there will at least be an action against him for fraud.

Anyone who finds anything belonging to someone else lying around and takes it with a view to profit is liable for theft, regardless of whether or not he knows who is owner – and if he does not know whose it is, his action is none the less theft. But if the owner of property has abandoned it, it cannot be stolen even if I intend to steal it, for there can be no theft when there is no one to steal from; and in our case there is no theft against anyone – indeed this is in accord with the opinion of Sabinus and Cassius, that as soon as we abandon anything it immediately ceases to be ours.

But if the thing was not really abandoned, the taker will nevertheless not be guilty of theft if he believed that it was. However, if it was not abandoned and the taker did not believe it either, but he found it lying about and took it, not to profit by it, but to return it to the owner, he is not liable for theft.

Next let us consider the case where the finder does not know who is owner, but takes the property just as anyone

might who intended to give it back to whoever might claim
it or prove that he was owner. Should he be liable for theft?
I do not think so. After all, people often do this sort of thing –
publish an advertisement that they have found whatever it is
and they will return it to the owner when he asks for it.People
like this show clearly that they have no theftuous intentions.
What then of someone who asks for a 'reward', as it is
called? Even though it is not really proper to ask for anything,
such a person does not seem on this account to be guilty of
theft.

In his twelfth book Celsus raises the following question: if
someone, of his own accord, deliberately throws something
away but without intending to abandon it and you take that
thing, are you liable for theft? His view was that if you
thought he had abandoned it you would not be guilty. But if
you did not think that, Celsus thinks it would be a doubtful
point – though he inclined to the view that you would not be
liable, because, he says, a thing cannot be dishonestly pur-
loined from him who threw it away of his own volition.

But if when cargo has been thrown overboard from a ship
someone appropriates it, is he guilty of theft? The question in
this case too is whether or not the owner intended to abandon
it. If he threw it out with the intention of abandoning it –
which is to be believed in most cases, because he knows it will
perish – he who finds it becomes owner without any question
of theft. However, if the owner did not have such an intention, but hoped to have it if it survived, he who found it must
give it up; and if the finder knows this and so has a dishonest
intent, he will be liable for theft. But on the other hand if his
intention is to keep the things safe for the owner, he will not
be liable. And if he believes simply that the cargo was jet-
tisoned and nothing further, he is again not liable.

Even if I become a half-owner of a slave who had previously
stolen something from me, the better opinion is that my right

of action is gone although I have only bought a part share, because if someone had from the outset been a part-owner of the slave he would not have had a right of action. Clearly, however, if I acquire a usufruct in him after the theft, it must be said that the right of action is not extinguished, because a usufructuary is not an owner.

44. (POMPONIUS) If a person who falsely claims to be a creditor's authorized agent is referred by the debtor to a third party and receives payment from him, he is liable to an action of theft by the debtor and the money paid belongs to the debtor.

If I give something of mine to you, believing it to be yours, whereas you know that it is properly mine, the better view is that this is theft on your part if you did this intending to profit dishonestly.

If a slave who is part of a deceased person's estate, and was freed in the will of his late owner, steals some part of the inheritance before the heir has entered upon it, he is liable to an action for theft because at no time was the heir his owner.

45. (ULPIAN) If a partner steals something belonging to the partnership (for he can indeed steal such things) it must be said that there is no doubt whatever that an action of theft is available against him.

46. (ULPIAN) All the authorities agree that even if the stolen thing ceases to exist, nevertheless the action of theft still lies against the thief. Thus if a slave who had been stolen dies, the action of theft still retains its force; nor will manumission of the slave cause the action to be extinguished. (Manumission is of course akin to death in so far as it takes the slave out of the ownership of his master.) Thus it appears that no matter in what way the slave is taken out of the ownership of his master, he still has the right of action in theft against the thief, and this is the rule we use; for the action lies not simply to the extent

that he is now out of possession but because he was at any time deprived of his services by the thief's doing. The same rule applies in the case of a *condictio*: that form of action is also available against a thief even if the stolen thing has in some way ceased to exist. The same is also true in respect of goods which have fallen into the hands of the enemy – it is the law that the action of theft can still be brought; and again, even if the owner abandons his rights of property after the theft, he can none the less bring the action.

If a slave held in usufruct is stolen, both the usufructuary and the owner have rights of action for the theft. These rights are divided between the two of them – the usufructuary sues in respect of the loss of his beneficial use, that is for whatever was the value of his interest that the theft should not occur (and this is doubled); the owner sues in respect of the interest he had in not being deprived of his rights of proprietorship. What we have said about double the value of the interest must also be understood to include four-fold damages in the case of red-handed thefts. The action is also available for someone who has the bare right of using the slave's services for whatever might be the value of his interest.

Again, let us consider the situation when this slave is pawned as security for a debt. It happens that even the pawnbroker has a right of action for theft. So too has the debtor, provided his interest in his slave is more than the amount which he owes.

To such an extent is it true that the actions of possible plaintiffs are independent of each other that if any one of them settles his loss with the thief, the better view is that only his own action is compromised and the others remain unaffected. This is just like the case where a slave owned by several masters in common is stolen and one of the joint owners settles with the thief – the other owner who did not settle still has the action of theft.

The owner also can sue the usufructuary of his property if he gives cause by concealing something which is properly the owner's or keeping it to himself.

It is rightly said that no one who thinks the owner consents to his dealing with the thing is guilty of theft; for how does a person deal dishonestly with a thing when he thinks the owner is in agreement, whether his belief be sound or unfounded? A person is only a thief if he tampers with a thing in the knowledge that its owner would not consent.

Take the converse case: I think that I am doing something without the owner's consent when in fact he is agreeable. The question is: do I commit theft? Pomponius says that I do; but the truth is that if the owner is agreeable to a course of conduct even though the other party does not know it, that other will not be liable for theft. If a stolen thing returns to its owner's control and then is stolen again, the owner will have a second action for theft.

47. (PAUL) If the ownership of stolen goods should be changed by any means whatsoever, the right to sue for theft is the new owner's, be he an heir, a possessor of goods in good faith, a father making an adoption, or a legatee.

48. (ULPIAN) A man who lost a silver vase brought an action for the theft of it. When there was an argument about its weight and the plaintiff had put it too high, the thief produced it in court – and the plaintiff (the owner) carried it off, while the thief was nevertheless ordered to pay damages of twice its value. This judgement was absolutely right, for the thing itself does not enter into account in a penal action, be it an action for red-handed or for 'ordinary' theft.

A man who knows a thief, regardless of whether he points him out or not, is not himself a thief, for there are many differences between actually concealing a thief and merely failing to point him out. One who simply knows is not liable for theft, but he who conceals a thief is so liable by virtue of this very fact.

It is clear beyond doubt that a person who takes in a slave at his master's request is neither a thief nor a kidnapper: how can anyone possibly be called a thief when he has the owner's consent? But if the owner objected and he took the slave regardless, he is still not a thief if he did not have the intent to conceal him, though he is if he did. Therefore he who takes a slave in without concealing him is not a thief, even if he does it against the master's wishes. However, we accept that an owner can prohibit that of which he does not actually know, that is to say, when he does not give his consent.

If I hire your services to clean my clothes and, without my knowledge or even against my will, you lend them to Titius and then they are stolen from Titius, you have a right to sue the thief because you are liable for their safekeeping; and I have a right to sue you because you should not have lent them and by doing so you committed theft. This is a case where a thief can sue for theft.

If a slave-girl is pregnant when stolen, or becomes pregnant while stolen, the child, when born, is stolen property and regardless of whether at the time of birth the thief still has her, or she is with a possessor in good faith. However, in this latter case no action lies for the theft of the child. But if she conceives and also gives birth when she has passed to a bona fide possessor, it happens that the child is not only not stolen property, but that it can be acquired by *usucapio*.

Foals of stolen mares become immediately the property of anyone buying the mares, and properly because they are accounted amongst natural proceeds – but the child of a female slave is not so reckoned. However, the general rule with regard to their young applies to all animals kept in herds.

When a thief sold the stolen property and the owner

wrested the purchase money from him by force, the view was
properly stated that he too had committed theft – indeed he
would even be liable to an action for robbery (by force),
because no one is in any doubt that the proceeds realized
by selling stolen property are not themselves deemed to be
stolen – therefore the money in this case, which represented
the stolen goods, was not itself a *res furtiva*.

49. (GAIUS) From time to time it happens that someone who
has an interest in property being kept safe cannot sue if it is
stolen. Thus a creditor cannot bring an action in respect of
property stolen from his debtor, even though as a result the
debtor cannot repay his debt – of course I am not speaking of
where the debt arises by the law of pledge. Again this rule
applies in the case of dowry property which is at the wife's
risk: it is the husband who can bring action, not the wife.

50. (ULPIAN) In an action of theft, the unit of damages which
is doubled or quadrupled is not the value of the plaintiff's
interest, but the actual value of the thing stolen. But if the
thing shall have ceased to exist by the time the action comes
on for hearing, an order as to damages will have to be made
just the same. The same is true also if the thing should have
dropped in value by then – in such a case the valuation is made
at the time of the theft; but if it should have become more
valuable, the assessment to be doubled would be the increased
value, because it is true to say that it was indeed a stolen thing
at that time.

Celsus says a man commits theft by helping and advising
not only when his intent is to enable his colleagues to commit
a theft, but also where, without that specific intent, he does
have an unlawful object. Pedius says very truly that just as no
one can commit theft without dishonest intent, neither can he
be guilty of theft 'by help and advice' without that same
intent.

A person is guilty of abetting theft by advice if he persuades someone else to commit theft or urges him on or provides him with information; he abets him with help if he provides assistance and co-operation in carrying off the property.

When a man holds up a red rag and chases cattle off so that they fall into the hands of thieves that is theft if he did it with dishonest intent; but even if he did not do it with theft in mind, such a pernicious pastime as this should not go unpunished and so Labeo says that an *actio in factum* should be allowed in such a case.

51. (GAIUS) Of course if cattle are driven over a cliff an *actio utilis* on the analogy of the Lex Aquilia lies in respect of the wrongful damage caused.

52. (ULPIAN) If anyone gives help or advice to a wife on taking her husband's goods, he will be liable for theft. But if he commits theft together with her, he will be guilty of theft though she is not. And if she herself gives help to the thief she will not be liable for theft but for the removal of goods. However, if her slave steals her husband's goods for her there is no doubt that she is then liable.

The same rule applies to a son of the family while he is doing his military service; for he cannot be guilty of theft against his father, though he may incur liability through a slave who is part of his *peculium castrense* if such a slave steals from his father.

But if my son who has a *peculium castrense* commits theft against me, it is worth considering whether I can bring some sort of *actio utilis* against him since he has the means to pay the damages. It could certainly be argued.

Let us consider on the other hand whether a son can sue his father if he takes some part of his *peculium castrense*. I think he can. If so he can accordingly not only commit theft against his son but can also be liable in an action for theft.

If a creditor does not return an article pledged with him when the debt has been paid off, Mela says he is liable for theft if he retains it with dishonest intent, and I believe this is a sound view.

If there is a bed of sulphur in a field and someone digs up some of the soil and carries it off the landowner can sue him for theft; and then, if the land is let, the tenant can sue on his lease to get the proceeds of the action handed over to him.

If your son or slave takes in clothes for cleaning and they are stolen, can you bring an action for theft? The answer is that if they are solvent you can bring the action; but if they have no resources, it must be said that an action does not lie at your suit. Furthermore, if someone buys a stolen thing in innocence and it is stolen from him, he has a right of action for the theft from him.

Labeo reports a case where a man told a corn-merchant to deliver a certain measure of corn to whoever came and asked for it in his name. A passer-by hearing this being arranged went and asked for the corn on the account of that other person, and it was given to him. A theft action lies against him who asked for the corn at the instance of the corn-merchant, not me, because he did that piece of business on his own account, not mine.

If someone claiming to be his owner gets a magistrate or whoever has the relevant authority to release my runaway slave from prison or other custody, is he liable for theft? It seems that if he gave sureties, an action should be given to me against those who let him go to compel them to assign their action against the sureties to me. But if they did not take sureties and handed him over to the applicant as the apparent owner, I as real owner have an action of theft against the false applicant.

Anyone who knocks gold or silver coins (or anything else) out of someone else's hand is only liable for theft if he did it in order for someone else to pick them up, and that other carries them off.

If someone carries off a lump of silver belonging to me and makes goblets from it, I can bring an action against him for theft or for a *condictio* in respect of either the lump of silver or the goblets. It is the same choice in the case of stolen grapes, or their juice or the skins: an action lies for theft, and a *condictio* too.

A slave who swears he is a free man in order to get a loan of money does not commit theft, for he has done no more than hold himself out as a creditworthy person. It is the same where a *filiusfamilias* makes out that he is a *paterfamilias* in order to get a loan the more easily.

Julian writes that if I give a man a sum of money to pay off a debt of mine and he, happening to owe that sum to the same creditor, uses it to pay his own debt, he commits theft.

If Titius sells something that does not belong to him and receives the purchase money from the buyer, this is not deemed to be theft of the money.

If one of two partners in a total partnership takes some article as security for a debt and that thing is then stolen, Mela says that only the one who accepted the security can proceed for theft and not the other one.

No one can commit theft by any use of words or writing, for we use the rule that theft is not committed unless there is some improper meddling with property. Accordingly, the giving of aid and advice alone does not matter – to attract liability it must be followed by some unlawful handling.

If someone drives my stallion ass among his mares so that they might get in foal, he is not guilty of theft unless he had theftuous intent. I wrote this in reply to an inquiry sent to me from Dalmatia by my pupil Herennius Modestinus about some stallions which a man was said to have turned in with his own mares – that he could be liable for theft if he did that with theftuous intent: anything less, and an *actio in factum* should be brought.

When I decided to lend money to a certain man of substance called Titius, you introduced me to another Titius, a person of no means, though you said he was rich, and after I had handed over the money you shared it with your Titius. You are liable for theft because it was done with your aid and advice – and of course your Titius is also liable for theft.

When you were buying goods by weight, someone fixed you up with some overweight weights. Mela writes that that person is liable to the vendor for theft, and you too, if you knew, for you did not accept the goods from a willing vendor because he was mistaken about the weight.

Mela also says it is theft if someone persuades my slave to erase his name from, say, a written record of his purchase, and I agree with him.

But if my slave is persuaded to make copies of my account books, I think an action for corrupting him lies against whoever it was who persuaded him to do it; but if that person does it himself, I should have an action for deceit.

If a string of pearls is stolen, it should be stated how many there were. Again, in an action for theft of wine, it is necessary to say how many jars were stolen. Whenever vessels are stolen, it is necessary to say how many.

If a slave of mine, who has freedom to dispose of his *peculium*, comes to an agreement with someone who had taken some item which he had not intended to give away, this seems to be a proper compromise, for although only the slave's owner could have brought an action for theft, the benefit of the *peculium* is nevertheless the slave's. Furthermore, if the whole penalty of double damages is paid to the slave, there is no doubt that the thief goes free. The consequence of this is that if perchance the slave receives from the thief whatever seems proper in the circumstances of the case, there is again a valid compromise of the action.

If someone takes an oath that he has not committed a theft, and then later handles the allegedly stolen thing, the action of theft can still not be pursued, though of course the owner can sue for the recovery of the thing.

If a slave is stolen and later instituted as someone's heir, the plaintiff can recover through his judgement for the theft even the value of the inheritance itself in case the slave should die before taking up his inheritance on his owner's instructions. It is the same if a claim of restitution is made after the slave is dead.

If a conditionally freed slave, or a thing left by way of legacy on condition, is stolen, and the condition in either case be fulfilled before entry is made upon the inheritance, an action for theft cannot be brought because the heir no longer has any interest in those items: but while the condition is yet unfulfilled they should be valued at what they would fetch on sale.

53. (ULPIAN) If a man robs an unoccupied house, he can be sued in an action for rapine for four times the value of the goods taken – but not for manifest theft, at least if no one catches him red-handed.

54. (PAUL) A person who breaks down the door of a house intending to perpetrate an insult will not be held guilty of theft even if things are carried off from the house by others, for the offences are characterized by the intent and disposition of the delinquent.

If a slave who has been lent steals something and the borrower is solvent, Sabinus says that the action on loan is possible against the borrower, as also is the action for theft against the owner in the name of the slave. But if the money demanded by the owner be paid, the action for theft disappears;

the same is true if the owner waives his action on the loan. But if your own slave steals something which you have borrowed, there will be no action for theft against you, the thing being at your risk; but only the action for loan will lie.

One who applies himself to the affairs of another will not have the action on theft, although the thing would be lost at his risk; but he will be condemned in the action for unauthorized administration only if the owner cedes to him the action for theft. The same is to be said of one who acts as a tutor or of a tutor who owes a duty of care, for instance, a tutor being one of several named in a will who, having given due security, undertakes sole administration of the ward's estate.

If you hold something of mine because a third person gave it to you and I take it away, Julian says that you could have the action for theft against me, only if you have an interest in retaining possession of it; instances would be that you defend the donated slave in noxal proceedings or give him attention when sick, so that you would have a good ground for retaining the slave against one asserting title to him.

55. (GAIUS). A pledgee who makes use of the property pledged with him is guilty of theft. It has also been held that he who lends someone else something which he has himself borrowed is liable for theft. This seems clearly enough a case of theft where he turns the use of another's property to his own profit. Nor is it an answer to this point that he did it without a positive intention to make a profit, for it is a form of profit when a man is generous with property that is not his and thus puts someone else under an obligation to do him a good turn. From this it follows that he who takes someone else's goods to give them to a third party is also guilty of theft.

The Law of the Twelve Tables does not permit us to kill a thief who is caught by day unless he defends himself with a weapon. The word weapon however means swords, sticks, stones – indeed anything which can be used for wounding.

Since the action for theft is appropriate for inflicting a penalty, whereas a *condictio* or the *vindicatio* are for the recovery of the stolen property, it is clear that if the thing has been got back, the action for the penalty can still be brought even though the *condictio* and *vindicatio* are dead; just as, conversely, when only the double or four-fold penalty has been paid, the *condictio* and *vindicatio* are still available.

If someone lends iron tools knowing they are to be used in breaking down a door or opening a chest, or knowingly lends a ladder for a thief to climb up, then, even though his advice was not a primary factor in the commission of the theft, he is liable to an action for theft.

If a tutor who is looking after his ward's affairs, or a curator, makes a compromise with a thief, the right to sue for theft dies.

56. (ULPIAN) When a creditor takes away property pawned with him, he is not considered to make a fraudulent dealing, but simply to avail himself of the pawning arrangement.

57. (JULIAN) Sometimes a thief incurs a further liability even while still under his penal obligation, so that an action for theft can be brought against him several times on account of the same property. An example occurs if the cause of possession is changed, as for example when the owner may have recovered his property and then the same thief steals the same thing again, either from the same owner or from someone to whom he had lent it or sold it. Furthermore if the personality of the owner is changed, the thief incurs a new liability.

He who brings a thief before the chief of police or the governor of the province is considered to have made his choice as to the means of seeking recovery of his property; and if the matter is thereby brought to a conclusion and judgement is given against the thief, the thing restored or the stolen money recovered, the whole question of the theft is settled, especially if the thief is not only ordered to restore the stolen property but also to suffer some additional punishment. But even if the judge orders nothing more than restitution, the very fact that the thief brought before him was in danger of some severer penalty is to be understood to bring the whole question of the theft to a conclusion.

If an item which was part of a slave's *peculium* is stolen but later comes back into the slave's possession, the taint of theft is removed and for this reason the thing is again part of the slave's personal belongings and thus in the possession of his owner. However when a slave himself removes some part of his *peculium* with theftuous intent, its legal character does not change so long as he retains it, for in such circumstances it has not been taken out of his owner's possession; but if he passes it to someone else, he commits theft.

A tutor who actually runs his pupil's affairs can settle an action for theft with the thief and if the stolen property is returned to his possession it ceases to be 'stolen goods' because the tutor is in position of owner; and the same may be said of the guardian of a lunatic, who represents the personality of the mad owner so closely that he is deemed to pass ownership of the lunatic's property by handing it over. Furthermore, a tutor and a guardian of a lunatic can recover stolen goods by a *condictio* brought in the names of their charges.

If two slaves of yours steal a suit of clothes and a piece of silver and you are sued on account of one for the clothes and the other for the silver, you will have no defence in the case about the silver on the ground that action has already been given against you for the clothes.

58. (ALFENUS) If a man digs a pit to dig chalk and carries the chalk away, he is a thief, not because of his digging but because of his carrying away.

59. (JULIAN) If theft is committed against a son in his father's

family, it is right that he can bring an action on that account when he becomes independent. Similarly, if goods which he has hired are stolen, he can likewise sue when he is a *paterfamilias* himself.

60. (JULIAN) If a man lends a thing and then secretly takes it back, it is not possible to bring an action of theft against him, because it is his own property that he recovered – and the borrower is freed of the contractual liabilities of the loan. This rule must be understood subject to the proviso that the borrower had no special right of retention, as for instance he would have if he had incurred necessary expenditures on the borrowed property; then it would be in his interest to keep hold of it rather than sue on the contract of loan. Because of this interest he can bring an action for theft.

61. (AFRICANUS) A runaway slave-girl is deemed to commit theft of herself; and she makes her child stolen property by handling it.

62. (AFRICANUS) If a slave owned in common by several owners steals from one of them it seems right that the action used to wind up partnerships should be brought and that the decision of the judge should include an order for the defendant either to make good the loss or give up his share in the slave. From this it seems to follow that if one co-owner disposes of his share, the action can be brought against his purchaser in the same way – just as a noxal action attaches to the wrongdoer personally. But Julian says we should not push the analogy to the extent that we would say the action could be brought against the slave himself if he became free – just as the action could not have been brought if he had been the complainant's own slave and not owned in common. From this he says it therefore appears that if the slave is dead the plaintiff cannot gain anything on this account, unless perchance some part of the stolen property has come to one of the co-owners. He says that from this it also follows that if you

pledged your slave with me as security for a loan and he commits theft against me, I can sue you by an action on the contract of pledge and get a decision against you in the same way either to compensate me for my loss or else surrender the slave to me on account of his offence. The same must be said about a slave whose sale had been agreed, but subject to a possible rescission of the deal. Therefore, just as the buyer would be obliged to hand back any accessions and profits made through the slave, so also the seller would have to pay compensation for any loss or hand over the slave himself to discharge his liability. But the law may provide even further: if for example the owner knowingly pledges a slave whom he knows to be a thief with a pledgee who is ignorant of this fact, he will be compelled to make good all loss however caused without the option of surrendering the slave – for this much is required by good faith. In an action on a sale, however, we must above all look at the warranty the seller gave as to the slave's character. But if the action arises out of a contract of mandate, Julian says he is in doubt whether this too might be a case where the defendant would have to make good any loss without the chance of the alternative and that even more so in this case than in the others mentioned above, the person who gave the mandate to buy the slave who proved to be a thief will, even though he was ignorant that he was a thief, nevertheless be obliged to make good the loss, for he who was the purchasing agent may very fairly allege that he would not have incurred the loss if he had not undertaken the mandate – and this point comes out even more clearly in the case of a contract of deposit for safekeeping. He grants, moreover, that it seems equitable that a man should not have to suffer loss through a slave's doings beyond the value of the slave himself – so it is even more just that no one should suffer because of a good turn done solely for the benefit of the person with whom he made a contract and with no advantage to himself. Therefore, just as in the above cases – sale, hire and pledge – it is maintained that it is the deliberate dishonesty of him who keeps back the information he has that should be punished, so also in this case fault on the part of the person who benefits under a contract ought to be at his expense only, rather than fall on the other party. It certainly was the fault of the person who gave the mandate in that he commissioned his agent to buy such a slave as the one described above – and it is the same in the case of the man who deposits a slave for safe-keeping because he was not more careful in warning the other party about the slave's character. It is not unreasonable that the rule should be different in a contract of free loan for use, because after all in that case the only person who gets any benefit is the borrower who asks for the use of the slave. Therefore, the lender, just like a hirer, will have to make good any loss occasioned by his fraud; but if he is not dishonest he will not forfeit anything beyond the slave's value. Indeed, even so the term fraud is being interpreted rather freely, as Julian says, because the lender is getting no benefit from this arrangement. I think all the above is true provided there is no fault on the part of the party who undertook the agency or safe custody; but the case is quite different if he of his own choice entrusts, say, plate or money to someone else's slave when the owner himself would never have done so.

I let a farm to you and, as is the usual custom, it is agreed that the produce should be my security for payment of the rent. If you should then secretly cart it off the farm, Julian says I can sue you for theft. Again, if you should sell such crops before they are gathered in and the purchaser takes them away, we submit that they become stolen property, with all that that implies, for the fact is that crops, as long as they are attached to the soil, are deemed to be part of the land and therefore whatever the tenant gathers in becomes his because he is held to do it with his landlord's consent. However, this certainly cannot properly be said of the present case, for by what reasoning can the produce possibly be said to become the tenant's when the purchaser takes it on his own account?

A *statuliber* who was directed by a testator to become a free man on payment of 10 *aurei* was defended in a noxal action by the testator's heir (when he had committed theft). While the case was being heard he paid 10 *aurei* to the heir and thus gained his freedom; and the question was asked whether the case against the heir could be dismissed other than by his handing over to the plaintiff the 10 *aurei* he had received. The opinion given was that it all depended on where the money came from. Thus, if it came from a source other than the former slave's *peculium* the heir would no doubt have to hand it over because, if the slave were not yet come to his freedom, he would himself have been handed over and the money would also have to be given to the plaintiff to whom he would himself have been surrendered. On the other hand, if it came from his *peculium*, the decision would be the opposite because the slave would have given the heir what was already his own money and the heir would not have allowed him to be in a position to have given this to the plaintiff.

63. (MARCIAN) A man who points out his route to a runaway slave does not thereby commit theft of the slave.

64. (MACER) The governor of a province has no power to prevent a conviction of theft bringing infamy on the defendant.

65. (NERATIUS) A testator appointed Titius as his heir and left a slave as a legacy to Seius,[11] but before Titius entered into his inheritance the slave stole some of his property. If thereafter Seius still wishes to have his legacy Titius can sue him for the theft on the part of the slave, because he did not yet belong to Titius when he committed the theft and, however much some would argue that as the slave himself becomes the property of the person from whom he stole that would put

an end to the right to sue and that the right would not revive even if he were transferred to someone else, in this case he did not even belong to Titius after he entered into his inheritance because the law is that things left as legacies pass directly from the testator to the beneficiary.

66. (ULPIAN) He who dishonestly handles someone else's property with intent to gain is a thief – and no less so if he later gives it back having changed his mind, for no one expunges his existing guilt by repenting of his offence.

67. (PAUL) If he who has given a thing as a pledge sells it, he commits a theft even though he is still its owner. This applies whether he has already handed it over to the creditor or has only so far entered into the agreement, and Julian agrees with this view.

If a man from whom a thing has already been stolen leaves it to me as a legacy while it is still in the hands of the thief and the thief thereafter meddles with it again, shall I have a right of action for theft? According to the opinion of Octavenus the action is available for me only and the heir has no right to sue on his own account because, regardless of the reason why ownership of the thing changed, it is the present owner who is competent to sue for theft.

The old lawyers held that he who maliciously summoned a mule-driver to answer a case in court would be liable for theft if the mules came to grief meanwhile.

Julian gave the opinion that a slave who was employed to collect debts for his master would be liable for theft if he continued to collect them after being granted his freedom. The same can be said also of a tutor who collected payment of a debt after his pupil came of age.

If you recommend a certain Titius to me as a man to whom I could safely lend money and I make inquiries about this Titius but you then bring along someone else to me as if he were Titius, you commit theft because I believe that man to be that selfsame Titius – at least if he who is brought along is aware of the situation; if he is not, he will not commit theft nor will you who brought him along seem to be aiding and abetting a theft because no such offence is committed. However, you will be liable to an *actio in factum*.

If I make a verbal contract of stipulation with you that 'nothing shall be done on your part to impede the handing over of the slave Eros to me by the first of the month', although I have an interest in his not being stolen (because if he is, you are not liable under our agreement, provided, that is, that you did not do anything to impede the transfer), nevertheless I cannot bring an action for theft.

68. (CELSUS) No one commits theft by denying that a thing was left with him for safekeeping, for theft is not committed by the denial itself, although it comes close to it; but if he takes possession of it with intent to convert it to his own use, he does then commit theft. Nor does it make any difference whether he wears a ring on his finger or keeps it in a jewel box if, when it was left with him for safekeeping, he appropriates it for himself.

If you had promised to pay a penalty in case of failing to deliver something by a certain date and that thing was stolen from you, so that you had to pay the penalty, the amount of that loss will be included in reckoning the damages in the proceedings for the theft.

A stolen slave-child grew up in the thief's household. The thief is deemed to have stolen the adult just as surely as he stole the child, though it is all one case of theft. Accordingly he is liable for twice the highest value the slave ever had while he was in the thief's household. But since he can only be sued once for the theft, how does that apply to the foregoing case? Just suppose for instance that the stolen slave had been stolen again from the thief and that he recovered him from the second thief. In such a case even if the first thief might have committed two thefts, he could not be sued more than the once. Nor do I doubt that in our original case it is the value of the adult rather than the child which ought to be taken into account. What could be more ridiculous than that the thief's position should be better the longer the theft continues?

When a sale of a slave is rescinded it is not possible for the purchaser to bring action against the vendor in respect of theft which the slave committed after the date of the sale but before the time when he was returned.

If a stolen slave steals from the thief who stole him, it is held that the thief can sue the slave's owner on that account, so that the misdeeds of such slaves should not go unpunished and also so that they should not be a source of profit to their owners – for very often the *peculia* of such slaves are increased by their thieving.

If after the expiry of his lease a farmer harvests the crop of the next year against the wishes of his landlord, it is worth considering whether he can be sued for the produce and the vintage. There seems to me no doubt at all that he is a thief and that if he has consumed what he stole he can be sued for its value.

69. (MARCELLUS) Julian maintained that the assets of a deceased person were not susceptible of theft in the time between the deceased's death and the heir's entry into his estate, except those things which the deceased had pledged or lent

70. (SCAEVOLA) or things in which someone else had a usufruct.

71. (MARCELLUS) Julian thought that in those cases the deceased's property could be stolen and that *usucapio* would be suspended and that accordingly the heir could bring an action for theft.

72. (JAVOLENUS) If someone borrows a thing and then appropriates it he is liable to actions both for theft and on the contract of loan. However, if he is sued for theft the action on

the loan is extinguished; and if he is sued on the loan he will have a defence to a further action for theft.

A man who takes possession of a deceased person's property before the entry of the heir cannot sue for theft in respect of any such property which is stolen, even though he could acquire ownership of such property by *usucapio*. The reason for this is that the party who can sue for theft is the one who has an interest in the thing not being stolen and in the eyes of the law that party is the one who would suffer actual loss through the theft rather than the one who would merely lose an expectation of gain.

73. (JAVOLENUS) Sempronia drew up a written statement of her case ready to hand to the centurion[12] for him to send to the appropriate office, but she never handed it to him. Lucius however read it out in court as if it had been properly handed in, but it was not in the office nor had it been given to the centurion. I wonder what charge should be laid against someone who dared to take such a statement from a private house and read it out in court when it had never been handed in in the usual fashion? Modestinus gave the opinion that if he took it surreptitiously he committed theft.

74. (JAVOLENUS) If he who accepts property as a pledge sells it although nothing was agreed about selling it, or, in a case where there is such an agreement, he sells it before the due date, he thereby makes himself liable for theft.

75. (JAVOLENUS) Attius stole from my possession a slave-woman whom I had bought in good faith for 2 *aurei*, not knowing that she was stolen property. Both the true owner and I sue Attius for theft and I wonder how the damages of each of us are to be assessed. The answer is: the buyer's damages are twice the value of his interest and the owner's are twice what she is worth to him. The fact that damages are due to two parties should not affect the answer for, indeed, the damages due to them both are assessed on the same principle:

the buyer gets the value of his possession and the owner the value of his ownership.

76. (POMPONIUS) If a man pretending to be someone else's agent induced me to make payment either to himself or to someone else to whom he delegates the collection, I cannot sue him for theft because there is no physical thing involved which was handled with dishonest intent.

77. (POMPONIUS) Someone who borrows something or undertakes to look after it safely and then uses it in some way other than as agreed will not be guilty of theft if he does this believing that the owner would not mind. Nor will he incur any liability under the contract of deposit for safekeeping; but whether or not he might be liable on the loan will depend upon his degree of fault, that is, in this case, whether he could reasonably have believed that the owner would have permitted him to do as he did.

If a man steals another's property and someone else steals it from him, the owner can bring an action against the second thief, but the first thief cannot, because it is the owner and not the first thief who has an interest in the safety of that property. This is the view of Quintus Mucius and it is quite right, for although the first thief has a sort of interest in the property's safety because he may be liable in an action to return it or its value, nevertheless an interest upon which an action of theft is founded must be an honest interest. We have not adopted the opinion of Servius, who thought that if no one appears as owner, nor seems likely to appear, the first thief could then take action, for even then a person is not understood as having an interest who will be making an improper gain. The owner will accordingly have rights of action against both the thieves, so that if he starts proceedings against one of them, he still keeps his right to sue the other; and he also has an action for recovery against both, because they are liable on distinct grounds.

78. (POMPONIUS) A man who takes a purse containing money is also liable to action for theft of the purse even though his dishonest intent was mainly directed at the money rather than the purse.

79. (PAPINIAN) A man handed over some property for inspection by someone else; if the inspector accepted also the risk of keeping it safe he can bring the action of theft if it is stolen from him.

80. (PAPINIAN) If a debtor takes back an article which he pledged he will by no means be able to recover what he has to pay in damages in an action of theft.

81. (PAPINIAN) If I sell a slave and before I hand him over he is stolen through no fault on my part, the better view is that it is I who can sue for the theft. It seems that it is I who have the necessary interest, either because I was owner at the time or because I would be liable to assign my right of action.

When a right to sue for theft is available through right of ownership, the question of what the thing is worth must still be settled by reference to its value to me (assuming I have no further special interest) for a man has no right of action at all unless he has some interest and this rule is illustrated in the case of *statuliberi* and legacies left to them conditionally. If any different principle were applied it would be impossible to make any assessment at all readily. Therefore the valuation is made simply by reference to what the use of the thing is worth to the plaintiff only in cases where a right of action of theft is given to a person who is not owner, because in those cases it is not possible for the action to proceed on the basis of the value of the physical thing itself.

If I bring an action for the production of things in court in order to exercise an option left to me as a legacy to choose from among a household of slaves, one of which has been stolen, it is the heir who has the right to action for the theft.

He has the requisite interest, and it matters nought why he has the obligation to keep them all safely.

Since a robber necessarily commits theft, he should be deemed a manifest thief, but he who instigates robbery is not liable to an action for theft but for robbery.

If Titius ratifies the acts of a false agent who accepts money on his account which was not owed to him, he can bring an action of agency against the dishonest party and the person who made the payment that was not due can sue Titius for unjust enrichment and will also have a *condictio furtiva* against the dishonest agent. However, if he chooses to sue Titius first, Titius cannot unreasonably make use of the defence of pleading fraud against him and thus oblige him to assign his right to bring a *condictio furtiva*. On the other hand, if the money really was owing, the debtor loses his right to sue for theft as soon as Titius ratifies the action of the agent because he is freed of his debt. The false agent would only commit theft of the money if he assumed the name of some genuine agent of the creditor and thus a debt owed to someone else. This rule applies equally to the case of someone who asserts that money is due to him as the heir of Sempronius (a real creditor) although he is in truth someone quite different.

Someone who was conducting Titius's business for him paid money on his behalf to a pretended agent of a creditor and Titius ratified the payment. A right of action for theft does not arise for him, even though it does for the payer as soon as he hands over the money, because Titius was not then owner of the money, nor was it in his possession. Titius will, however, have a right to recover what was paid in error and the man who handed over the money can proceed by *condictio furtiva*. The judge will require him to assign this right to Titius if he should bring action against Titius for any matters arising out of the conduct of his affairs.

82. (PAPINIAN) For theft of civic funds there is liability for theft rather than embezzlement of public money.

83. (PAUL) A fuller or tailor who takes in clothes to clean or mend but then wears them would seem to be guilty of theft on the ground of wrongful meddling, because he did not take them for that purpose.

Both the landlord and the tenant farmer can sue for theft of crops taken from the farm because they both have an interest in recovering them.

A man who carries off for immoral purposes a slave girl who is not a prostitute is guilty of theft and, furthermore, if he keeps her hidden away he is liable to punishment under the Lex Fabia.[13]

Anyone who steals accounts and securities is liable for theft up to the amount of the sums recorded; nor does it matter whether the accounts are cancelled or not, because it can be proved from them that the money paid was owed.

84. (NERATIUS) If anyone takes possession as supposed heir of the property of someone thought to be dead but who is actually alive, he does not commit theft.

A person who has an action of theft brought against him on his own account and another on account of the separate acts of his slave will not be granted leave to plead the defence to those charges that the alleged theft was the joint act of them both.

85. (PAUL) Although a stolen thing cannot be acquired by *usucapio* unless it shall first have returned to its owner, nevertheless, if its value has been assessed in an action for its recovery, or if the owner has sold it to the thief, the correct view now is that there is nothing to prevent *usucapio*.

86. (PAUL) He who has an interest in property not being stolen has the right of action for theft, provided he held the property with the consent of its owner as, for example, in the case of a man to whom something is hired. On the other hand, he who willingly manages someone else's property, for example as a

tutor or curator, does not have the action in respect of property which is stolen as a result of his own neglect. Again, a man to whom a slave is owed under a formal promise or as a legacy does not have a right to sue for theft even though he has some interest; and it is the same in the case of a surety for rent owed by a tenant farmer.

87. (TRYPHONINUS) If something that was stolen or taken by force in a robbery returns into the hands of its former owner without his knowledge, it does not appear that it has come into his power again; accordingly, even if it is sold to a bona fide purchaser after a recovery of possession of this sort on the part of the owner, *usucapio* cannot follow.

88. (PAUL) The action of theft is available to a creditor for the amount of the pledge stolen rather than the amount of the debt. However, where the debtor himself stole the pledge the rule is otherwise, so that the damages for such a theft include the whole sum of money owed, plus the interest on it.

89. (PAUL) If a plaintiff sues for robbery he cannot sue for theft as well; but if in a robbery case he chooses to bring the theft action for double damages, he can also sue for robbery provided his total claim does not exceed four times the value of the property in question.

90. (PAUL) If a freedman or client steals from his patron, or a hired servant from his employer, that does not give rise to an action for theft.

91. (JAVOLENUS) A cleaner (from whom a customer's clothes had been stolen) was released by the owner from his liability under the contract for the hire of his services. Labeo correctly says he has no right to sue for the theft. Furthermore, if the cleaner should already have sued the thief before the customer brought action against him on the contract of hire and then, before the theft action came to judgement, he was released from his liability under his contract, his own action against the thief would have to be dismissed; but if the customer had not

granted such a release, the thief would have to be found guilty. In all these cases the reason is that the cleaner only has a right of action to the extent that he has an interest.

No one can be found guilty of giving aid or advice to another who is himself incapable of forming the intent of committing theft.

92. (LABEO) If a man, when he knows that something of his is being stolen, does nothing to prevent it, he cannot sue for theft. (PAUL) But, on the contrary, if a man knows his property is being taken and submits because he cannot prevent it, he can bring an action; and indeed, even if he could do something to stop it but does nothing, he can still sue. This is how it happens from time to time that a patron steals from his freedman, and so also may someone who is regarded with great respect steal from a person who is so overcome with awe when in his company that he cannot resist.

93. (ULPIAN) It must be remembered that nowadays it is usual to bring criminal proceedings in cases of theft and that the complainant signs a criminal charge, not because the proceedings are on a state charge but because it seemed right to keep a check on frivolous charges by threat of punishment out of the ordinary. However, no one is any less free to bring a civil action if he so chooses.

CONCERNING
ROBBERY WITH VIOLENCE
AND RIOTOUS ASSEMBLY

❖

1. (PAUL) Anyone who seizes property by force is liable to an action of non-manifest theft for double damages and to an action of robbery with violence for quadruple damages; but if the action for robbery is brought first, the action for theft will be refused. However, if the theft action is proceeded with first, the other will not be refused, though only damages beyond those recovered in the first action will be awarded.

2. (ULPIAN) The Praetor says: 'If any damage is alleged to have been committed maliciously and with evil intent against anyone by persons unlawfully assembled, or property is said to have been seized by violence, I will grant an action against whoever is said to have done this. Furthermore, if it is alleged that a slave has committed such acts I will grant a noxal action against his master.'

In this Edict the Praetor has been mindful of offences which involve violence. If anyone can prove that he has suffered violence he can proceed by a public criminal action against violent offences, and some authorities hold that the private action should not be decided before the criminal proceedings; but it seems to be more readily available and although the case should be heard first under the Lex Julia concerning private violence an action ought not to be refused to those who choose the private prosecution.

It is not only he who perpetrates robbery with violence who acts 'maliciously' and with evil intent (in the words of the Edict) but also he who according to his previously formed plan collects together armed men for the same purpose. Therefore it is not only the man who actually assembles the band together, but also he who makes use of armed men already got together by someone else for the purposes of robbery with violence, who is considered to have acted with malice aforethought. In this context we should understand 'men got together' to mean men assembled specially to commit the offence. No mention is made of any particular sort of men, so it matters not whether they be slave or free. Moreover, if only one accomplice is involved we still speak correctly of 'men got together'; and again, if you put the case where only one man actually commits the offence, I do not think the words of the Edict fail to cover that case also, for when it refers to 'persons unlawfully assembled', it means that whether he acts in concert with others, armed or not, who assembled for the purpose, he will still be liable under this Edict.

The mention of dishonest malice includes violence, for he who resorts to violence acts maliciously; but on the other hand, he who is malicious does not always necessarily resort to violence. Thus malice is one thing and violence is another and he who commits an offence without using violence himself but by deceitfully inciting others is equally included.

The Praetor speaks also of 'damage'. This includes every kind of injury, even that which is clandestine. However, I do not think all clandestine damage is included, but only that which is combined with violence; and thus one is correct in one's law to say that a person who commits damage alone and without violence is not included in the terms of this Edict, but that if it is committed by people got together, even without violence provided they act with malice, it will come within the terms of the Edict.

Furthermore, neither the action of theft nor the action under the Lex Aquilia are incorporated into the terms of this Edict, even though sometimes they have much in common with it. Julian writes that he who commits robbery with violence is a more shameless thief, and that he who causes damage with the aid of persons assembled together can also be held liable under the Lex Aquilia.

'Or property is said to have been taken by violence.' When the Praetor says 'property taken by violence' we understand it thus: that it applies even when only one article has been seized by force.

A defendant who does not himself get men together but is found among them and either takes something by force or causes some damage will be liable under this action. But it has been asked whether this Edict refers only to damage caused fraudulently or violently by persons got together by the defendant, or whether it also includes robbery with violence or damage committed by the men referred to although they may have been assembled by someone else. The better view is that this is included as well, together with any harm caused by persons assembled by another, so that he who assembled them, as well as he who merely joined them, would both seem to be liable.

In this action the whole price of the property within the relevant year is quadrupled as the measure of damages, not merely the value of the plaintiff's interest in it.

The action can also be brought with reference to a household without the necessity of showing which particular men of that family committed the robbery or did the damage. The term 'household' also includes the slaves, that is those engaged in its service even though they may claim to be free men, or the slaves of others who are serving us in good faith. I do not think it possible for the plaintiff to use this action to proceed against a master on account of a number of his slaves individually, because it suffices for the master simply to pay four times the amount claimed once and for all. However, under this action noxal surrender should not be made of the whole household of slaves but only of those (or that individual) who are proved to have acted maliciously.

These proceedings are commonly called the action for robbery with violence. Only a person who has acted with malicious intent is liable to this action. Therefore anyone who resorts to force to seize what is his own will not be liable for robbery with violence, but he will be dealt with in a different way. So too, anyone who seizes by force his own slave who is possessed in good faith by someone else will similarly not be liable under this action because he removes his own property. What then if he seizes something with a mortgage on it in his favour? He will be liable.

The action for robbery with violence will not be granted against a child below the age of puberty who is not capable of forming a criminal intent unless it is alleged that it is his slave, or a group of his slaves, who committed the offence, in which case he could be liable to a noxal action for the surrender of that slave or group of slaves for the robbery.

If a tax collector drives away my cattle because he thinks I have committed some infringement of the tax laws I cannot, says Labeo, sue him for robbery even if he is mistaken because he is lacking any fraudulent intent. However, if he shuts them up so that they cannot feed and they die of hunger an *actio utilis* will lie against him under the Lex Aquilia. On the other hand anyone who shuts up cattle which he had taken by force will be liable to the action on that account.

In this action we do not merely look to see if the property concerned belonged to the plaintiff; for whether it did or not, if he had any connection with it he will have grounds to bring the proceedings. Therefore if it is lent or let to me, or pawned with me or left with me for safekeeping, so that it is my con-

cern that it should not be taken away, or if I am bona fide
possessor of it or have a usufruct or any other right in it so
that it is in my interest that I should not be robbed of it, it
must be said that I have the right to bring this action, which
lies not to recover ownership but to allow me to recover my
property, that is to say any part of my assets. It must also be
observed that, generally speaking, I can also sue in theft in all
the above cases when the taking is done secretly. So I am
entitled to that action in such circumstances, though some
would argue that we do not have a right of action for theft in
respect of property left for safekeeping. But on that point I
have added 'if it is in our interest that the thing should not be
seized by force' and in such a case I now have an action for
theft, provided that in a case of deposit for safekeeping I have
accepted liability for negligence or have received the value
of the thing deposited other than as a payment. It is useful to
observe that even when there may not be an action of theft in
respect of a thing deposited for safekeeping action can be
brought for robbery, because there is no small difference
between an offender who steals secretly and one who commits
robbery with violence – the former does at least conceal his
offence, the latter not only publishes his but even commits it
publicly. Therefore when a person proves he has even a
minimal interest in the property involved he should be able to
bring an action for robbery.

If a runaway slave of mine buys some things for his own
use and they are taken from him by force, I can bring an action
for robbery because those things are my property.

When property is taken by violence an action can be brought
for theft or for wrongful damage, or proceedings may be
instituted either for its value or for the specific recovery of
each article.

This action is granted to a man's heir and to other successors;
but it is not granted against heirs and other successors because

penal actions do not lie against them. However, let us see
whether it should be granted in respect of any property by
which they have been enriched. I think that the Praetor did
not promise that this action would lie against heirs in respect
of property they inherit, because he thought that personal
proceedings for its value should suffice.

3. (PAUL) If a slave committed robbery and action was
instituted against him after he had been freed, even though
the action could have been brought against his master it cannot
be brought against the slave after his manumission, because,
regardless of the fact that it is possible to sue other people, the
plaintiff will fail in his action against him. Furthermore Labeo
says that if action is instituted against the master within the
available year after the offence and then another is started later
against the slave after he has been freed, he will have a defence
on the ground that the matter has already been tried.

4. (ULPIAN) The Praetor says: 'In the case of anyone alleged
to have committed unlawful damage maliciously as one of a
mob, I will grant an action against him for double damages,
provided the proceedings are started within a year of the
right to sue arising; after that year has elapsed I will grant an
action for simple damages.'

This Edict is promulgated to deal with damage caused by
any member of a disorderly crowd. Labeo says that the term
'crowd' means any sort of riotous assembly and that it is
derived from the Greek word for making a tumult. How
many, then, do we agree make a 'crowd'? If two people are
quarrelling we shall not acccept them as constituting a crowd,
for two people cannot reasonably be said to make any sort of
mob. However, if there are more, say ten or fifteen men,
they can be called a crowd. But suppose there are three or
four? That is not a crowd. Labeo very rightly points out that
there is a great difference between a tumult and a mere
quarrel, because a tumult is the uproar and upheaval made

by a multitude of men whereas only two may make a quarrel.

This Edict applies not only to a person who causes damage as one of a mob but also to anyone who acts maliciously to bring it about that a mob does cause damage, whether he himself is then present or not, for malice can indeed make its presence felt even if the person concerned is not there. It must also be said that if someone joins a crowd by chance and then incites the doing of damage, the Edict applies to him as well, provided he was present at the time as one of the crowd and had the requisite evil intent, though on these facts it cannot be denied that the crowd did the damage because of his malicious incitement.

If a man on arrival excites a crowd and incites it to an unlawful object by his shouts or by any act such as making accusations against someone or even by arousing pity, and if damage is committed as a result of his malicious incitement, he will be liable, even if he did not originally have the intent of getting the crowd together; for there is no doubt that the damage was caused by the crowd being excited through his malice, and the Praetor does not require that the defendant should have got the crowd together, but only that the damage should result from the malicious incitement of one of the members of it.

There is this difference between this Edict and the one mentioned earlier: in the first one the Praetor refers to damage committed maliciously by people assembled riotously and to robbery with violence done by people who are not part of a crowd; but in the second Edict he deals with damage committed maliciously by a crowd where the defendant did not gather the crowd together but where it was incited by his cries or inflammatory language, or because he aroused pity. Here he is liable even though someone else assembled the mob, because he himself was part of it.

Accordingly, because of the seriousness of this sort of thing the first Edict provides for a penalty of four-fold damages and the second stipulates double damages. However, they both grant the right of instituting such proceedings only within one year of the alleged offence, and after that year has elapsed action will only lie for single damages. Moreover, the second Edict only mentions damage suffered and property lost and makes no reference to robbery with violence; but no matter – action can be brought for robbery under the first Edict. Property is said to be lost in this context when it has been left by anyone and destroyed – for example cut or broken to pieces. This is an action *in factum* and is granted for double the value of the property, calculated by reference to its true value, estimated at the present time, and is always doubled if the action is brought within a year. The plaintiff must prove that the damage was caused by a mob; if it was caused in any other way this action will not lie.

If when Titius struck my slave a crowd collected and as a result my slave lost something, I can sue the person who struck him even though it was the crowd that caused the loss – that is of course if the defendant started it by striking him so that the loss might result. However, this action will not lie if there was any other reason for striking the slave. On the other hand, when a person gathers a crowd together himself and beats a slave in front of the crowd in order to do him an unlawful injury rather than with intent to cause loss, the Edict will apply, for it is true that he who causes unlawful injury shows malice and that he who shows an intent to cause damage is responsible when it occurs.

The Praetor will grant the action against a single slave or against a whole household of slaves. What we have already said above about heirs and other successors being entitled to sue for robbery with violence also applies here.

CONCERNING
INSULTING BEHAVIOUR
AND SCANDALOUS LIBELS

◆

1. (ULPIAN) Anything which is done unlawfully is called 'injury', for everything which is done otherwise than according to law is deemed to be injurious; and this is the general meaning of the term. Here are some further examples: damage caused by negligence is sometimes referred to as injury, in the general sense, and we are in the habit of using the term in this way for the purposes of the Lex Aquilia; at other times we speak of injustice as an injury, for in cases where someone pronounces a judgement inequitably or unjustly an injury is said to arise because it is without law or justice and thus not lawful.

But in a more particular sense the term 'injury' is used to indicate an outrageous insult. The term 'insult' is derived from the verb 'to despise'.

Labeo says that an 'injury' in the above sense may arise either from something done or from words. By 'something done' he means with the hands; by words, when the hands are not used, as by insult.

Every insult is either inflicted upon the person or relates to someone's dignity or dishonour. Insult is, for example, inflicted upon the person when someone is beaten; it relates to dignity when a lady's attendant is abducted and it tends to disgrace when modesty is violated.

Again, a person may suffer an insult either on his own account or through others – on his own account when the outrage is perpetrated against the *paterfamilias* or mother of a family; and through others when there is a natural succession, as where it is directed against my children, my slaves, my wife or my daughter-in-law – for an insult reflects on us when it is directed against anyone who is in our family or entitled to our affection. And if perchance an outrage is perpetrated upon the corpse of a deceased person, if we are his heir or possessors of his effects, we can on our own account bring an action for the insult; for the insult to the deceased reflects upon our own honour. The same applies if it is the reputation of him whose heir we are which is attacked. Furthermore, any insult perpetrated upon our children is also a reflection upon our own honour, to the extent that even if someone sells a son with his own consent, his father may bring an action for the insult, even though the son is not competent to sue because no insult is perpetrated upon him who consents to it.

Whenever the funeral or the corpse of a deceased testator is insulted after his heir has succeeded him, it must be said that it is in a way an insult to the heir, for it is always in the heir's interest to preserve the testator's reputation untarnished. If the outrage to the deceased occurred before the heir succeeded to the estate, the right of action accrues to the estate and is thus acquired by the heir through inheritance. And lastly Julian writes that if the body of the testator is detained before the heir has entered upon the estate there is no doubt that the actions will accrue for the inheritance. He also thinks that the same will apply if any insult is done to a slave of the estate before the entry of the heir, for the action passes to the heir from the estate.

Labeo writes that if, before the heir has entered, someone lashes a slave belonging to the estate who has been given his freedom by the will of the deceased, the heir can bring an action for the outrage, but if he is thrashed after the heir has made his entry, the slave himself can bring the action, regardless of whether or not he knew at the time that he was freed.

Neratius writes that whether or not the insulter knew that his victim was my son or wife, I have a right to sue him in my own name. Neratius also says that sometimes three rights of action may arise from one outrage and further that one person's right to sue is not extinguished when another sues. Take the case for example of an insult to my wife who is still a daughter in her own family: a right of action lies not only for me and for her father but also for my wife herself.

2. (PAUL) If an insult is inflicted upon a husband, his wife cannot bring an action because it is right and proper that wives should be defended by their husbands, but not husbands by their wives.

3. (ULPIAN) It is said that those who can suffer an insult can equally well commit one. Granted, there are some who cannot commit one, such as, for example, madmen and infants, who are not capable in law: such persons may suffer an outrage but cannot perpetrate one. For it is the essence of outrages that they are done intentionally; so we must say it follows that if such persons even resort to blows or defamation, they do not seem to have committed an outrage. Thus one may suffer an insult without perceiving it, but cannot commit one without knowing of it, even though he may not know precisely who it is directed at. Therefore, if someone strikes another person for a joke or in sport he will not be liable, nor if he beats a freeman he thought was his slave.

4. (PAUL) Nor if I, intending to strike my slave with my fist, should unwittingly hit you when you were standing near by.

5. (ULPIAN) The Cornelian law of outrage provides for the case of the person who wishes to bring action because he

claims that he has been struck or beaten or that his house has been entered by force.

This law also provides that no one can preside as judge who is son-in-law, father-in-law, stepfather, stepson, cousin or is any more nearly related to the plaintiff by consanguinity or affinity, or is his patron, or the father of any of the persons already mentioned.

The Lex Cornelia gives an action for three causes: where someone is struck, or is thrashed or his house is forcibly entered. Thus it seems that any injury which can be inflicted by hand is within the scope of the Cornelian law.

According to Ofilius there is this difference between striking and beating: to beat is to inflict a blow in anger, but mere striking does not imply infliction in anger.

In the context of this law we understand by 'house' not only one which is owned by the plaintiff, but where he happens to have his home; and so the law applies regardless of whether he lives in his own house, or in one which he rents or indeed where he lives free; or even if he is just there as a guest.

What if someone lives in a country seat or place surrounded by gardens? The same should apply. And if the owner lets a farm and it is entered by force, it is the tenant and not the landlord who can bring the action.

But when anyone enters the land of another, who is tending it for the owner, Labeo says it is not the owner who can bring the action under the Lex Cornelia, because he cannot have his home everywhere – that is, in all his houses. I think this law applies to every house which is the home of the head of a family, even though he may not actually be living there. Let us consider for example the case of someone who goes to Rome to study: he has not made Rome his home and so it should be said that if his home is entered by force, the Cornelian law would still apply. To this extent therefore it does not apply to temporary lodgings nor to pothouses, though in other cases it may apply to those who live in a place for more than a brief spell, even though they do not make their homes there.

The question is put whether when a son *in potestate* has suffered an injury the head of the family may sue under the Lex Cornelia; and it seems that he cannot, though the father may bring the action granted by the Praetor while the son brings action under the Lex. Indeed a son still in his father's family can bring action under any of the heads covered by the Lex Cornelia, even without warranting that his father approves his action; indeed Julian writes that a son who brings action for outrage under any other laws cannot be compelled to give any assurance of his father's approval. By this law the plaintiff may tender the oath so that the defendant can swear that he has committed no insult. Sabinus in his writings on Assessors says that even the Praetors have to follow this rule, and indeed it is so.

If someone composes, writes or publishes something tending to bring another into hatred, ridicule or contempt, or maliciously causes this to be done, even though it be published in the name of another, or even anonymously, he can be sued under this law and if he is found guilty, he will be declared to be untrustworthy so that his word cannot be given in court, nor can he make a will. And by a Decree of the Senate the same fate awaits anyone who publishes any scurrilous epigrams or anything else of the like, even in shorthand, and anyone who offers such things for sale or purchase. Any free person or slave who gives evidence leading to the successful prosecution of such persons will be rewarded according to the means of the accused person in the judge's assessment; and in the case of a slave, maybe he could even be freed – and why not if some public good comes of his action?

6. (PAUL) This decree of the Senate is a necessary addition to

the law for those cases where the name of the person who suffered the wrong is not given; then, because proof is difficult, the Senate wishes the offence to be dealt with by a public inquisition. On the other hand, if his name is given he can bring an action in the normal way according to the common law; nor should he be prevented from getting judgement in a private action which is prejudicial to a public proceeding, because the case relates to private matters. It is clear that if a public proceeding is instituted, a private action will not be allowed, and vice versa.

7. (ULPIAN) The Praetor's Edict says: 'Anyone who brings an action for outrage must say precisely what injury has been done,' because he who brings an action which may result in public disgrace should not be vague over a critical matter for someone else's public reputation but he must define and specify precisely the wrongful injury which he alleges he has suffered.

If it is said that a slave has been killed to cause an insult, why shouldn't the Praetor allow the public action to give way to the private one under the Cornelian law, just as if someone wished to bring an action because you administered poison for the purpose of killing the slave? So he would act more justly if he did not grant the public action in a case of this sort. However, it is our custom to maintain that in cases where there is a public action we should not be prevented from bringing a private proceeding. This is indeed true but only where it is not the main object publicly to prosecute for punishment. What then shall we say of the Lex Aquilia, for this law is mainly concerned with the public prosecution of a penalty and not primarily with the death of the slave? For its concern is the loss caused to the owner; but in an action for outrage the proceedings are to avenge murder or poisoning itself rather than make amends for the loss. What then if someone seeks to bring action for outrage because he has been hit on the head with a sword? Labeo says he should not be prevented from suing, for he says this is not an action which concerns the public; but this is not right, for who can doubt that the defendant can be sued under the Lex Cornelia?

A further reason for stating precisely the nature of the plaintiff's injury is so that we may know what sort of insult it was and whether judgement might have to be given against a patron on account of his freedman. For it is important to remember that an action for insult is not always, but only from time to time, given to a freedman against his patron, in those cases where the insult suffered is gross – the sort of treatment only meted out to slaves. For we allow a patron a right of reasonable chastisement of freedmen and the Praetor will not hear a freedman's complaint of an insult which he claims to have suffered unless he is moved by its exceptional severity. For the Praetor should not put up with yesterday's slave who is today's freedman complaining that his erstwhile master spoke to him roughly or struck him lightly or corrected him. But if he was scourged or severely beaten or seriously wounded, it would be entirely proper for the Praetor to intervene on his behalf.

If one of his children who is not *in potestate* wishes to bring an action against his father, the action for insult should not be allowed lightly, but only if the atrocity of the outrage is the persuading factor. But it is clear that the action is not available to someone subject to paternal authority, even though the outrage be atrocious.

When the Praetor says, 'Whatever is the cause of action must be clearly stated,' how is this to be understood? Labeo says a person speaks 'clearly' when he makes his statement of claim without ambiguity (unlike those who say 'on the one hand but maybe on the other') and alleges that he has suffered a specific injury.

If you inflict several outrages on me – if for example you get together a disorderly mob and enter my house, so that I am at the same time both beaten and insulted – the question arises whether I can bring separate actions against you for each outrage. Marcellus, following the view of Neratius, approves of joining together in one action all the injuries that a person has suffered at the same time.

Our Emperor has said in a Rescript that at the present time we can proceed in a civil action even in atrocious cases, by which we mean those which are graver and more insulting than usual. Labeo says that an insult may be deemed atrocious by reason of its place or timing, or the person insulted. An insult becomes more atrocious in respect of the person when committed against a magistrate or a parent or patron, and in respect of time when committed in public during the games. He also says it matters greatly whether the insult is committed in the presence of the Praetor or in private, because it is much more serious if done in public; and that it may also be atrocious by its very nature, as for example when a wound is inflicted or someone is hit in the face.

8. (PAUL) The gravity of the wound makes it atrocious and sometimes the part affected, as where an eye is pierced.

9. (ULPIAN) While we are considering insults atrocious by their very nature, and granted that it is atrocious when inflicted upon the person, there is still the question whether it can be atrocious when not caused to one's body, as for example when one's clothing is torn, or one's companion is abducted or outrageous language is used. Pomponius maintains that insult can be said to be an aggravated one even without a blow being struck, when the aggravation depends on the person insulted. But when someone strikes and wounds somebody in the theatre or the Forum he commits an aggravated insult even though the wound itself is not serious; and it matters

little whether it is a head of a family or a son in power on whom the injury is inflicted, for this is still considered an aggravated case.

If a slave causes an atrocious insult his master can be sued for it if he was present; but if he was not, the slave is to be taken before the Governor who will order him to be flogged.

If anyone makes lewd advances, be it to a man or woman, freeborn or freed, he will be liable for the outrage and even if an attempt is made on the chastity of a slave, this too is deemed to be an outrage.

10. (PAUL) The modesty of a person is said to be attacked whenever anything is done tending to deprave an otherwise virtuous person.

11. (ULPIAN) It is not only the perpetrator of an outrage, for example he who actually struck the blow, who is liable to an action; but anyone who aided and abetted is equally liable.

The action for outrage is based upon justice and equity, but the right of action is lost if the outrage is disregarded. If someone overlooks an outrage, that is, if someone, having suffered it, lets it pass from his mind, he cannot revive it if he later regrets having condoned it.

Hence, if any agreement about an outrage, or a compromise is made or any oath is exacted in court, an action for that outrage can no longer be pursued.

Anyone can bring an action for outrage either himself or through some representative such as an agent or guardian, or through any other such person who is accustomed to acting on behalf of others.

If an outrage is perpetrated against anyone else on my orders, most of the authorities say that both I, who gave the order, and he who acted on it are liable to an action. Thus Proculus rightly maintains that if I hire you to commit an outrage for me, proceedings can be brought against both of us for our offence, because the outrage was perpetrated at my instigation. He also says the rule is the same if I order my son to commit an outrage against you; but Atilicinus says that if I prevail upon someone to commit an outrage who would otherwise be unwilling to obey me, the action lies against me.

Although an action for outrage is not granted to a freedman against his own patron, it can be brought by the husband of a freedwoman, in her name, against her patron; for whenever a wife suffers an outrage, her husband is deemed to bring the action in her name, and Marcellus concedes this point. But more recently I have made a note that this cannot be said in every case – for just because she is married, why should reasonable correction or even strong language (short of the obscene) be denied to a freedwoman's patron? But if the woman was married to a freedman, we would say, by all means, that her husband ought to be allowed an action against her patron for an outrage; and this is a view with which many agree. From all this it seems that our freedmen can not only not sue us in respect of outrages they suffer themselves, but also cannot bring actions on behalf of those in whom they have an interest that they should not suffer in this way.

It is clear that if the son or wife of a freedman wishes to bring an action for outrage they themselves have suffered, they should be allowed to proceed, for the action is not granted to the father or husband on their behalf, since they can bring proceedings in their own name.

There is no doubt that anyone who is said to be a slave but asserts that he is a free man can bring the action against a defendant who alleges that he is his master. This is so whether the alleged master is trying to reduce him to slavery, or whether the slave is asserting his liberty, for we use this law without regard to such distinctions.

12. (GAIUS) When an action is brought to reduce anyone from liberty to slavery, and the plaintiff knows all along that he is a free man, nor is he doing this in the course of recovering some

of his own property by due judicial process, he is liable to an action for the outrage.

13. (ULPIAN) An action for outrage is not granted for or against an heir. The same rule applies when this wrong has been inflicted on my slave: in this instance too, the action for injury is not available for my heir. But once the action has been actually joined, it may be continued by one's successors.

He who proceeds by public law cannot be deemed to have caused an outrage thereby, for the execution of legal process cannot be deemed an actionable injury. Similarly, if someone is arrested for not having obeyed a Praetor's decree, he cannot on that account bring an action; but if anyone should bring me before a tribunal maliciously and simply to harass me I can sue him for the outrage.

If someone will not suffer a person's case from being heard when public honours are being considered – for instance if a statue or some other such thing is involved – should he then be liable to an action for the injury? Labeo says not, even though he may have caused an insult; but he says it matters a great deal whether something was done deliberately to cause affront or whether he simply prevents an act from being done in honour of another.

Again, Labeo says that when one man had earned appointment as an ambassador, and the electing board gave the responsibility to someone else, he could not bring an action for injury on account of the labour he had put in; for it is one thing to impose a duty upon a person and quite another to inflict an insult upon him, and this rule should be adopted in the case of other offices and duties which are unjustly bestowed. Thus if anyone should pronounce such a decision for the purpose of giving affront, the same rule should apply, but no action lies in respect of any act of a magistrate performed by virtue of his judicial authority.

If someone prevents me from fishing or casting a net into

the sea can I bring the action for *iniuria* against him? Some
authorities say that I can, and they include Pomponius. The
majority, however, maintain that the case is the same as that
of a man who is not allowed to bathe publicly, or take a seat
at the theatre, or go into, sit down or associate with other
people in any public place, or indeed if anyone prevents me
from making use of my own property. In such cases the action
for *iniuria* can be brought. In olden days an interdict was
available to anyone who took a lease of public places because
it was necessary to prevent the use of force against him by
which he might have been stopped from enjoying his lease.

But what is to be said of the case where I prevent anyone
from fishing in front of my house or country seat? Am I
liable to an action for *iniuria*, or not? For the sea, just like the
seashore and the air, is the common property of all men, and
it has often been stated in rescripts that no one can be prevented from fishing, nor from bird-catching – except that he
can be prevented from going onto someone else's property.
Nevertheless, it has been maintained, though quite without
legal authority, that I can stop anyone from fishing in front of
my house or country seat – accordingly someone so stopped
can sue for *iniuria* on that account; however, I can properly
prevent anyone from fishing in a lake which is my private
property.

14. (PAUL) It is clear that if anyone enjoys a private right to
any part of the sea he will be entitled to the interdict for protection of possession if he is hindered in the exercise of his
right, because this relates to a private rather than a public
matter, as enjoyment of a right based upon private title rather
than public right is involved. Interdicts are adapted to private,
not public, affairs.

15. (ULPIAN) A further question is put by Labeo: if someone
should turn the mind of another by some drug or other, will
an action for *iniura* lie? Labeo maintains that it does.

If a man has not been physically beaten, but hands have been threateningly raised against him and he has been repeatedly terrified that he was about to be thrashed, even though he was not actually struck, the assailant will be liable to an equitable extension of the action for *iniuria*.

The Praetor says: 'I will grant an action against anyone who raises an outcry against another contrary to good morals or who has caused this to be done.'

Labeo says that to raise an outcry amounts to *iniuria*. An outcry is said to consist in a tumult or in concerted vociferous abuse. When several voices come together it is called 'concerted vociferous abuse' when the voices are indeed concerted against the individual; but the requirement added by the Praetor, that it be contrary to good morals, shows that he takes cognizance not of every united clamour but only that which violates good morals and also tends to bring someone into hatred, ridicule or contempt. He also says that 'contrary to good morals' should not only be understood to relate to the standards of the offender, but must be taken to refer to the moral standards of the community in general.

Labeo says that the defamatory clamour of a mob of voices not only can be raised against a party who is present, but can also be directed against a person in his absence. Thus, if they come to your home, a clamour is said to be raised against you even though you are not actually there; and the same rule applies to your lodgings or your shop. And it is not only the person who himself joins in the shouting who is deemed to have raised a clamour against you, but also he who has instigated others to raise a tumult, or who sent them.

The words 'against another' were not added without reason, for if the clamour is not raised against some specific person, the offence is not committed.

If someone attempts to raise a clamour against a person, but it does not come about, he will not be liable.

From the foregoing it seems that not all abuse is technically a clamour, but only that which is bawled aloud; and as to whether one or many yelled such things, a clamour is only where such is done in concert. Whatever is said other than by yelling or in a crowd cannot properly be said to be a clamour, but is rather defamation.

If an astrologer or anyone else professing unlawful powers of clairvoyance is consulted and says that a person was a thief when he was not, an action for defamation cannot be brought against him, but he is liable under the Imperial Ordinances.

An action for *iniuria* which is based upon a clamour does not lie for or against one's heirs.

If anyone accosts young girls who are dressed as slaves he would seem to have committed only a minor offence – and less still if they are got up as prostitutes and not dressed like respectable mothers of families. Therefore if a woman was not (soberly) dressed in matronly clothes, anyone who calls out to her or who entices away her female companion is not guilty of *iniuria*. We must accept the term 'companion' to mean someone who accompanies and follows anyone, and, as Labeo says, they may be slave or free, male or female. Labeo defines 'companion' in this context as one who is appointed to follow someone around for the purpose of keeping him or her company, and it is the abduction of such a person either privately or in a public place which is *iniuria*; and teachers are included amongst companions. Labeo says further that the abduction is committed not at its outset but only when someone has actually removed the companion from the company of his or her master or mistress. Moreover, not only someone who employs force to do this, but he who simply persuades the companion to leave also seems guilty. And it is not only he who actually abducts the companion who is liable under the Edict, but also anyone who calls out to one of them or follows them around. To 'call out' for this purpose is to make improper suggestions or alluring proposals – this is not like raising a clamour, but it is contrary to good morals. He who simply uses foul language is not making an assault on anyone's virtue but he is liable to an action for the affront.

It is one thing to call out or accost someone, and another thing to follow them about; for he who accosts a woman attacks her virtue by his speech, whereas he who follows her constantly, even silently, dogs her steps. Such assiduous pursuit can be productive of a certain degree of dishonour. It must be remembered however that not everyone who accosts someone or follows her about can be guilty under this Edict (nor will he who does it as a merry prank or by way of rendering some honourable service come within the terms of this Edict), but only someone who acts contrary to good morals.

I think that a betrothed man should be able to bring the action for outrage, for any insult inflicted upon his intended wife is deemed to be an insult to him too.

The Praetor says: 'Nothing shall be done to bring a person into hatred, ridicule or contempt, and if anyone violates this rule, I will punish him according to the facts of the case.'

Labeo says this Edict is mere surplusage, for we can anyway bring a general action for *iniuria*; but it also appears to Labeo himself (and this is indeed correct) that the Praetor, having examined this matter, wished to make special mention of it, for it seems that when public acts do not have attention specifically drawn to them they tend to be forgotten.

Generally the Praetor forbade anything which would make someone infamous, so whatever anyone does or says which brings dishonour to someone else may give rise to an action for the insult. This is true of almost anything which brings disgrace on someone – as for example the malicious use of mourning dress or filthy clothes, or allowing the beard to grow unkempt, or the composing of scurrilous lampoons, or the publishing or singing of anything which casts aspersions on anyone's reputation.

When the Praetor declares, 'If anyone breaks this rule, I will punish him as befits the circumstances of the case' he should be understood to mean that he will consider fully all the relevant facts; that is to say that he will take into account both the personal character of the plaintiff who brings the action and the record of the defendant, and also the nature of the complaint itself and the particulars of the plaintiff's injury.

If anyone attacks another's reputation by making a complaint to the Emperor or to anyone else, the action for injury can be brought – so says Papinian. He also says that he who is prepared to sell the outcome of a case can, even before he is paid any cash, be condemned in an action for the outrage, and also suffer a whipping on the orders of the Governor – for it is clear that he has caused great insult to the person whose judgement he offered for sale.

When anyone takes possession of someone else's property, even a single article, in order to cause an affront, he will be liable to an action. Similarly if anyone gives notice of the sale of a pledge which he has received from me, in order to defame me (as a defaulting debtor), Servius says I can bring an action for the insult. Further, anyone who calls someone else his debtor when he is not, intending thereby to insult him, will also be liable.

The Praetor says: 'If anyone is alleged to have beaten the slave of another improperly, or to have had him tortured without his master's order, I will give an action against him. Likewise where any other similar thing is alleged, I will grant an action if proper cause is shown to me.'

If anyone injures a slave in a way which is also an injury to his master, I reckon that the master can bring an action in his own name. But even if he did not act intending to affront the master, the Praetor should not let the injury to the slave pass unpunished, especially if it was caused by torture or by beating – for it is clear that the slave suffered thereby. If however one of a number of co-owners beats a slave who is owned jointly, it is clear that he will not be liable to this action, because he acted within his rights as a master; but if a usufructuary does this, the master may sue him, as indeed a usufructuary may sue a master who thus infringes the contract of usufruct.

The Edict speaks of acts 'contrary to good morality' meaning that it is not everyone who strikes a slave who is liable, but only he who strikes him improperly, and so if anyone does so with the intention of correcting or reforming him he is not liable to action. And hence Labeo asks whether I could take action for the impropriety against a city magistrate if he wounded my slave with a whip. He says that the judge should find out what my slave had done which caused him to be whipped, for if the slave had made an impudent attack on his dignity or sneered at his badge of office, the case against the magistrate should be dismissed.

The verb 'to beat' is in this context not properly used in respect of blows with a fist.

We understand the word 'torture' to mean torment and bodily pain used to extract the truth; accordingly mere interrogation or a reasonable use of terror is not a subject for this Edict. However, we include in the term 'torture' such things as that called 'the bad quarters':[14] thus when interrogation is carried out forcibly and with the infliction of bodily torment, that is to be understood as 'torture'. Even if torture is inflicted on the orders of the slave's master, Labeo says that he too must be held liable if it exceeds the proper limits.

The Praetor's Edict also says: 'Where any other illegal act is alleged, I will grant an action if proper cause is shown.' Thus if a slave has been excessively beaten or subjected to torture, judgement can be passed against the guilty party without further inquiry; but if he has suffered some other sort of hurt, action will not lie unless proper cause is shown. Thus the Praetor does not promise the action on the slave's account for every sort of injury. For if he was only lightly struck or not grossly abused, he will not grant an action; and if he was defamed by any act or by any scurrilous verses, I think that the Praetor's inquiries should be widened to take account of the slave's own character, for it matters a great deal what sort of slave he might be, whether he was frugal, methodical and careful or whether he was a vulgar scullion or a lowly drudge or whatever – and what if he was shackled, a known bad lot or – the ultimate disgrace – branded? Thus it is that the Praetor must take account not only of the alleged injury, but also the character of the slave against whom it is said to have been perpetrated and it is in the light of these factors that he will allow or refuse an action.

Sometimes the injury done to a slave reflects upon his master, sometimes not; for if someone, thinking a slave belonged to someone else and not to me, beat that slave even though he maintained that he was a free man, and he would not have beaten him had he known he was mine, Mela says that I cannot sue him for an injury against me.

If anyone should start proceedings for insult because his slave had been beaten and later starts another action for wrongful damage, Labeo says that they are not the same thing because one action relates to damage done wrongfully, whereas the other arises from insult.

If I have the right of usufruct in a slave and you have the ownership of him and he is beaten or subjected to torture, you rather than I have the right to sue. The same applies if you have thrashed a slave whom I possess in good faith, for the master has a better right to bring the action for the insult.

Again, if anyone beats a free man who was in my service in good faith as a slave, it should be settled whether he beat him in order to insult me. If he did, I can bring an action. Again, therefore, an action lies with respect to the slave of another who was serving me in good faith whenever the injury was committed with the intention of insulting me, for we give the right of action to the master in the name of the slave. If however he touches or beats me the action lies on my own account – and the same distinction can be drawn in the case of the usufructuary.

If I cudgel a slave who belongs to several masters it is clear that they will all be able to bring actions for the insult to them all,

16. (PAUL) but, as Pedius says, it is not right that judgement should be given for a larger amount than the particular owner's individual share, so it is the judge's duty to work out the values of the different shares.

17. (ULPIAN) But if I did this with the consent of one of the owners, thinking that he was the sole owner of the slave, an action for insult will not lie for any of them; if however I knew that the slave belonged to several owners, no action will lie for the owner who allowed me to thrash the slave though it will lie for the others.

If torture has been inflicted by order of a tutor, guardian or manager, it must be said that the action for insult will not be available.

My slave was whipped on the orders of the magistrate before whom we were appearing through your doing or because of your plea. Mela thinks I should be granted an action for *iniuria* against you for whatever amount the court thinks fair. Furthermore Labeo says that if the slave should die his master can sue because the case then concerns loss to him caused by the unlawful insulting act. Trebatius agreed with this view.

Some sorts of insults might seem slight and of no impor-

tance when caused by free men, yet they are serious when
inflicted by slaves, for an insult increases in the light of who
it was who caused it. When a slave gives affront it is clear that
he commits an offence. It is reasonable therefore that a noxal
action should be granted in such circumstances in respect of the
harm suffered, but, if he prefers, his master can bring the slave
to court and have him whipped and thus appease the insulted
party. It is not necessary for the master to show cause for his
whipping though he has power to say why he should be
whipped, or, if the aggrieved party is not satisfied by this,
the slave can be handed over by way of recompense, or the
amount of damages fixed by the court will have to be paid.
The Praetor's Edict says that damages are 'in the discretion
of the judge', so that he can fix the punishment according to
the standards of good and reasonable men. If before the master
produces his slave in court to be whipped to satisfy the
aggrieved party in pursuance of some decision of the court,
the plaintiff then changes his mind and insists upon bringing
action against the master for his alleged insult, his action
should not be entertained, for he who has received satisfac-
tion has had his affront settled; for if he had swallowed his
insult voluntarily it may be said with confidence that the
right of action for that insult would have been extinguished,
in just the same way that the right to sue for insult is annulled
by effluxion of time.

If a slave should cause an insult on the orders of his master,
the master can certainly be sued even in his own name; but if
evidence is given that the slave has been freed, Labeo says that
the action can lie against him because the blame attaches
personally to the wrongdoer and a slave is not obliged to obey
his master's every whim. But if he should kill anyone on his
master's orders we exempt him from the penalties of the Lex
Cornelia.

It is clear also that if he commits some offence in the defence of his master he has reason on his side and he has a good defence if he is prosecuted on that account.

If a slave in whom I have a usufruct commits an *iniuria* against me I can bring a noxal action against his owner. My legal position should not be any weaker because I have a usufruct than it would have been if I had not had that right. But the rule is otherwise if the slave is owned in common by several owners (including me) – then our law will not grant an action to another co-owner because he too is in part liable for the offence.

The Praetor's Edict says: 'If someone is alleged to have insulted someone who is under the control of another, and that person to whose authority he is subjected, or anyone else who can act on his behalf, is not in court, I will, provided good cause is shown, grant a right of action to the person who alleges that he has been insulted.'

When a son who is still under his father's power has suffered insult and his father was present but is unable to bring the action because of insanity, or on account of some other mental disorder, I think that the action still lies and in this sort of case the father is deemed not to have been present.

However, if the father is present but will not commence the action because he wishes to postpone or abandon it or even pardon the insult, the better opinion is that the right to sue should not be granted to the son, because in those cases when the father is absent the son is allowed to sue only because of the supposition that his father would probably have done so if he had been there.

Sometimes, however, we think that even if the father excuses the insult, the son should nevertheless still be allowed to sue, for instance if the father is himself a shady or depraved character whereas the son is a man of honour. The reason for this is that a father who is beneath contempt should not evaluate the insult to his son by his own debased standards – consider for example the situation where the father is a person for whom both law and reason would require the Praetor to appoint a legal guardian.

If, however, once the case has been brought before the court the father should go away or neglect to prosecute the case or proves to be grossly depraved, it must be admitted that the right of action should be conceded to the son if proper cause is made out. The same applies if it is shown that the son has been emancipated.

The Praetor gave preference to sue to the father's agents rather than to the insulted parties themselves. But when such an agent neglects the case, or is in collusion with the other side or is not able to sue those who committed the insult, the action will then be available to the complainant himself. Here we understand an agent to be not necessarily a specially appointed legal representative to plead the case – it is sufficient if the general care of the ward's property has been entrusted to him. However, when the Praetor says that if a proper case is made out he will grant an action to the party who was insulted, this must be understood to mean that when inquiry is made it must be shown how long the father has been away and when he is expected back, and whether the person who wants to sue for insult is dilatory or unbusinesslike to the point of uselessness, and on that account unfitted to bring the action. When the Praetor then refers to the party 'who has sustained the insult' this must be understood to mean that sometimes his father will be entitled to sue, for example in a case where a grandson suffered an insult and although his grandfather was not present his father was. Julian's opinion was that the action should be granted to the father rather than to the grandson himself, for he took the view that the father has a duty to protect his son whenever necessary even while the grandfather is still living.

Julian also says that a son should not only be able to bring an action himself, but could also appoint a solicitor to act for him; for otherwise, he says, it could happen that if we do not allow him a solicitor and he should be prevented by illness from getting to court, there would be no one to conduct the case and it must then be dismissed. He says furthermore that when a grandson suffers an insult and there is no one to conduct the case on behalf of the grandfather, the father should be allowed to do so, or to appoint a solicitor, for the right to have a solicitor is allowed to everyone permitted to sue in their own names. He also says that a son should be deemed to bring an action in his own name, because when a father fails to do so, the Praetor will allow him to sue.

If a son under his father's power brings the action for insult, the father is not competent to sue.

Julian also says that an action for insult is allowed to a son under his father's power when there is no one to act on the father's behalf and that in such a case the son is deemed to be head of the household. For this reason, if he has been emancipated or appointed an heir by a will, or even if he is disinherited or has refused his father's estate, authority is granted to him to conduct his case. It would be quite absurd that someone who might for proper cause be granted permission by the Praetor to prosecute an action even while under his father's power should be deemed incapable of avenging his insults after he had become head of a family, and that this right should be transferred to his father who had abandoned him in so far as it lay within his power to do so; or (which would be still more objectionable) if the right should be transferred to the father's heirs, who, without doubt, are in no way concerned with an insult inflicted upon a son under his father's power.

18. (PAUL) It is not right or just to condemn anyone for

bringing a guilty person into disrepute, for it is necessary and proper for the offences of guilty persons to be known.

If one slave causes an affront to another, an action should be brought just as if his master had been affronted.

If a married woman who is still subject to her father's *potestas* is insulted, both her husband and her father can sue for the affront. Pomponius rightly maintains that the defendant should be condemned to pay damages to her father in the sum that would have been payable had she been a widow, and to her husband in the same amount just as if she were independent, because the injury suffered by each party has its own separate valuation. Accordingly if a married woman is in no one's power she still cannot bring the action herself because her husband can bring it in her name.

If an insult should be inflicted upon me by someone who does not know me, or if anyone thinks I am Lucius Titius whereas I am Gaius Seius, the main issue will be the prime consideration, that is the fact that he intended to insult me; for I am a particular individual although he may think I am someone other than myself and therefore I shall be entitled to bring an action for the insult. But when anyone thinks a son under his father's power is the head of a family, he cannot be held to have insulted that person's father any more than he insults the husband when he believes a woman to be a widow, because in these cases the insult is not directly aimed at the father or husband personally, nor can it be transferred to them from the son or widow merely by thinking about it, because the intention of the insulter does not extend beyond the aggrieved party and he thought he was the head of a family. However, if he was aware that he was indeed a son in his father's power but did not know whose son he was, I would hold (so says Pomponius) that his father could sue on his own account, just as a husband can bring an action if he knew that the woman he insulted was married; for he who knows these facts intends to inflict an insult to the son or wife upon the father or husband whoever they may be.

19. (GAIUS) If my creditor, whom I am ready to pay, should molest my guarantors in order to cause affront to me, he will be liable to an action for the insult.

20. (MODESTINUS) It was his view that if Seia intending to cause an insult, sealed up the house of her debtor while he was away without the authority of the magistrate who has the authority to allow such a thing, an action for insult could be brought.

21. (JAVOLENUS) The assessment of damages for the insult suffered should not date from the giving of judgement but from the time when the affront was given.

22. (ULPIAN) If a free man is arrested as a runaway slave he can bring an action for insult against his captor.

23. (PAUL) Ofilius says that if anyone enters another's house against the owner's will, even though his object be to summon him before a magistrate, he will be liable to an action for the insult.

24. (ULPIAN) When anyone is prevented from selling his own slave he may bring an action for the insult he suffered.

25. (ULPIAN) If anyone should have sexual intercourse with a female slave, the owner can sue for insult; but if he hides the slave or does anything else with theftuous intent, he will also be liable for theft. If, however, he should ravish (and thus spoil) a young virgin girl slave, some authorities maintain that he would also be liable under the Lex Aquilia.

26. (PAUL) Whenever anyone makes a laughing stock of my slave or my son, even with his consent, I am still considered to have suffered an affront, as for example if he takes him to a tavern and gets him involved in playing dice; and this will always be the case when the person who persuades him does so intending thereby to insult me. However, it is possible for the

evil counsellor not to know who the master is, and so it becomes necessary to have an action for corrupting a slave.

27. (PAUL) If a statue of your father which was placed on his monument is broken by having stones thrown at it, Labeo says that the action for defiling a tomb will not lie, but an action for insult will.

28. (ULPIAN) The action for injury does not affect interests in property until the pleadings have been settled.

29. (PAUL) If you free or alienate a slave on whose account you are entitled to sue for an insult, you nevertheless retain the right to bring the action.

30. (ULPIAN) Who doubts that an action for an insult sustained during slavery will not lie after the slave has been freed?

If an insult has been inflicted upon a son, even though both father and son will acquire a right to sue, the measure of damages will not be the same for both,

31. (PAUL) for the insult may be greater to the son than to the father – if for example he is of superior rank to his father.

32. (ULPIAN) It is not allowed for magistrates to do anything which might cause insult, and so if a magistrate does cause an insult, either as a private person or in his official capacity, he can be sued for it. But can he be sued while he is still a magistrate or must the action wait until he has given up his office? The better opinion is that if he is a higher magistrate who cannot (except in a case of fraud) legally be summoned to court, it will be necessary to wait until he relinquishes his office. However, if he is one of the inferior magistrates, that is, one who does not have the highest power and authority, he can be sued even during his magistracy.

33. (PAUL) Anything done in accordance with good morality to uphold the interests of the state and causing insult to anyone will not be subject to action because the magistrate did not intend any affront, but was concerned to uphold the standing of public affairs.

34. (GAIUS) If a number of slaves jointly beat someone or raise a clamorous mob against him, each of them is individually guilty of the whole offence; and, of course, the insult is all the greater as it was committed by slaves. Indeed, there are as many insults as there are persons inflicting them.

35. (ULPIAN) When someone commits an atrocious insult and he can shrug off the judgement against him in an action because of his notoriety and indigence, the Praetor must prosecute the case with the greatest severity and punish all concerned in the insult.

36. (JULIAN) If I wish to bring an action in a son's name against his father, and the father appoints a solicitor, it is understood that the son is not defended unless he gives security against costs of the suit. Therefore an action should be given against him just as if he were not defended by his father.

37. (MARCIANUS) It is provided by Imperial Constitutions that anything placed upon public monuments to defame someone shall be removed. The action for insult can even be brought as a civil matter under the Lex Cornelia and the amount of damages will be in the discretion of the judge.

38. (SCAEVOLA) A decree of the Senate provides that no one shall carry about a statue of the Emperor to excite unpopularity. Anyone breaking this law shall be publicly put in chains.

39. (VENULEIUS) No one may wear filthy clothes or dishevelled long hair in public under the name of an accused person unless he is so closely related to him that he could not be compelled against his will to give evidence against him.

40. (MACER) The late Emperor Severus of blessed memory sent a rescript to Dionysius Diogenes as follows: 'Anyone who has been found guilty of an atrocious insult cannot be a member of the Decurian Order:[15] nor can it be of any help to you if a governor or anyone else who pronounces on this

matter, or indeed even those who oppose the established law
on this subject think that you remain a member of the Order.'

41. (NERATIUS) A father who has suffered an insult through
the person of his son should not be prevented from taking
action for his own affront and that of his son by two sets of
proceedings.

42. (PAUL) Litigants appearing before a judge should not raise
a clamour in court, or they will be branded with infamy.

43. (GAIUS) Anyone who brings an action of insult on false
evidence will be condemned in special proceedings – that is
to say he will suffer exile, deportation or expulsion from his
order.

44. (JAVOLENUS) If the owner of a house lower down makes
smoke in order to smoke out his neighbour higher up, or if
the owner of the upper house throws or pours anything down
onto his neighbour lower down, Labeo would have it that no
action can be brought for insult. I do not think he is right if
the reason for doing these things was to give affront.

45. (HERMONGENIANUS) At the present time it is usual in
cases of insult to pass sentence to suit the circumstances of the
case and parties involved in it. Thus in some cases slaves who
have been whipped are restored to their masters and free men
of the inferior classes are thrashed with rods, while others are
punished by banishment for a time or by denial of the use of
their property.

NOTES

◇

1. *Colluctatio* was wrestling, rather as we know it today. To the Greeks it was both a science and an art, so that not only did the contestants seek to win; they also sought to win gracefully and according to the precepts of the various schools. Like so much of their art, literature and architecture, the Romans adopted also the Greek styles and attitudes to wrestling. The two main styles were the upright, where one sought to throw one's opponent, three throws usually winning a bout, and ground wrestling, where the bout continued until one of the combatants conceded defeat. The Romans practised keenly in order to gain physical fitness generally and as an important part of military training.

2. *Pancratium* (πΑΝΚΡΆΤΙΟΝ): 'In the event boxing and wrestling were combined with kicking, strangling and twisting. It was a dangerous sport, but strict rules were enforced by umpires who closely watched the combatants. Biting and gouging were forbidden, but nearly every manoeuvre of hands, feet and body was permissible. You might kick your opponent in the stomach; you might twist his foot out of its socket; you might break his fingers. All neck-holds were allowed, the favourite method being the 'ladder-grip' in which you mounted your opponent's back and wound your legs around his stomach, your arms round his neck.' (F. A. Wright, *Oxford Classical Dictionary*, p. 775.)

3. Usufruct was a strictly personal servitude giving a specified person a right to use and enjoy the subject of the right and to take its fruits or income for himself, provided the substance of the thing remained unimpaired. Kaser suggests that it was of early origin dating from the days of the agricultural economy in order to provide maintenance for members of the family who were virtually disinherited by the rules of succession on the death of the *paterfamilias*, especially the widow and unmarried daughters. This he says, would account for its strictly

personal and non-transferable nature, even though it was later developed for a far wider range of beneficiaries. (See Kaser, *Roman Private Law* 29.1.1.) For a contrary view of the origins of usufruct see Buckland, *Textbook of Roman Law*, p. 268.

4. If a son *in postestate* or a slave committed a delict, the father or owner was liable for the penalty, but could avoid paying it by handing over the son or slave to the injured party (noxal surrender). The original idea was to allow the plaintiff to wreak personal vengeance on the wrongdoer, but this was inconsistent with the sovereign rights of the father's or owner's *potestas*. Eventually, therefore he was virtually given the choice of buying off the vengeance by paying the penalty or surrendering the wrongdoer to the plaintiff.

5. In English law an easement is a right over someone else's land (known as the servient tenement) such as a right of way or right of support which a landowner enjoys by virtue of owning his particular plot (called the dominant tenement). The Romans called these rights servitudes, as do almost all non-English lawyers.

6. The Twelve Tables gave an action (*actio de pauperie*) similar to a noxal action, whereby the owner of an animal which did damage would be liable either to pay compensation or to surrender the animal to the plaintiff. The action was available only where the damage was caused as a result of the animal acting out of character. It therefore probably did not apply to wild animals, since they were more or less expected to cause damage, but even if it did, the owner would not have been liable once such an animal had escaped, since he thereupon ceased to be owner of it. The Aediles, who were the magistrates responsible for markets and fairs and the safety of the streets, therefore forbade the keeping of wild animals, such as wild dogs, boars, bears or lions, near a public road and imposed penalties for contravention of this edict.

7. The text reads '10,000' and '20,000' without specifying the unit. It serves to make its point without. However, monetary units are referred to elsewhere. The most valuable of the Roman coins were the gold *aureus* and the half *aureus*; next the silver *denarius* and half-*denarius*, then the *sestertius* and *dupondius*, which were brass, and smallest of all were the *as* and *quadrans*, which were copper. 16 *asses* = 1 *denarius*; 25 *denarii* = 1 *aureus*.

8. The object of *vindicatio* was to recover property. *Condictio* was appropriate to recover the money value where the property was irrecoverable.

9. Justinian refers to this law in *Institutes* 4.18.10, as follows: 'Among the laws giving rise to public prosecutions [criminal actions] there is also the Lex Fabia, which inflicts capital punishment according to the imperial constitutions in certain cases, but lesser punishments in others.' Cicero also refers to this law (*Pro Rabirio*, 3) but nothing more is known of it.

10. Captured soldiers expected death, or at least to be enslaved; this was general in the classical world, and was reflected in the Roman law in that the legal position of a Roman citizen captured by the enemy was similar to that of a slave, though as a humane concession (deplored for example by Horace, who considered it decadent for captives to hope to return rather than face a 'manly' death (*Odes* III.5)) his rights remained in suspense ready for him to resume them, should he return to Roman territory. By right of *postliminium* the returning captive resumed his freedom and his rights just as if he had never been captured. In Justinian's law, marriage continued although the husband was a captive, but if he died in captivity he died a slave: but by a law of Sulla his will, if made before capture, remained valid.

11. Titius and Seïus (and their feminine forms) are the names normally used in giving examples referring to Roman citizens. Similarly, Stichus and Pamphilus are slave names.

12. The office or rank of centurion is best and most generally known in a military context. In later times however, the term is also used to indicate an officer of the court (see *Codex Theodosianus* 1.16.7) though it is unlikely to have been used in this way in the time of Modestinus. Jolowicz, however (*De Furtis*, p. 110), suggests that this usage here does not necessarily indicate an interpolation in the text, for a military officer might quite well have been employed by some tribunal in the time of Modestinus.

13. See p. 120 and note 9 above.

14. 'The bad quarters' (*Mala Mansio*) was a kind of punishment not unlike the rack, in which the victim was stretched out and tied fast to a board.

15. The Decuriones were the local councillors of the fully developed

Roman municipal system of local government. They were recruited from the ex-magistrates and by appointment by the censors at the quinquennial census. Once appointed they held office for life. Wealth, age, status and reputation were taken into account, though the minimum age of twenty-five was often overlooked in the cases of members of influential families, who were elected as a mark of respect to the family. From being an honour, the position later became a burden, for the Decuriones were made responsible for collecting the imperial taxes due from the municipality; moreover they were personally liable for any default of payment. This later became an intolerable burden and was a substantial contributory factor in the breakdown of the municipal system in the later Empire. A. N. Sherwin-White concludes that 'the Decurionate became an hereditary inescapable *munus* (public duty) of the wealthy, who degenerated from a ruling class to a tax-collecting caste known as *curiales*'(see *Oxford Classical Dictionary*, p. 318).

FURTHER READING

❖

Textbooks

The major statement of Roman law in English is to be found in W. W. Buckland, *A Text-Book of Roman Law* (3rd edition by Peter Stein, Cambridge University Press). This is a monumental work to which all subsequent accounts must necessarily be heavily indebted. Simpler accounts suitable for introductory reading are: Alan Watson, *Law of the Ancient Romans* (Southern Methodist University Press); Barry Nicholas, *An Introduction to Roman Law* (Oxford University Press); and J. A. C. Thomas, *Textbook of Roman Law* (North Holland).

General Background

A great deal of useful background material specifically related to the Roman Law is to be found in J. A. Crook, *Law and Life of Rome* (Thames and Hudson). Background matters specifically related to the reign of Justinian are to be found in P. N. Ure, *Justinian and his Age* (Penguin).

Historical Background to Roman Law

The standard work is H. F. Jolowicz and B. Nicholas, *Historical Introduction to the Study of Roman Law* (3rd edition by Barry Nicholas, Cambridge University Press). Other useful details are to be found in H. Kunkel, *An Introduction to Roman Legal and Constitutional History* (translated by J. M. Kelly, 2nd edition, Oxford University Press); and H. J. Wolff, *Roman Law* (University of Oklahoma Press).

Comparative Studies

W. W. Buckland and A. D. (Lord) McNair, *Roman Law and Common Law* (2nd edition by F. H. Lawson, Cambridge University Press) is a comparison in outline concerned with the fundamental rules and institutions of the Roman law and the common law, and examines the approaches of the lawyers of the Romans and the English to the same facts of human life. F. H. Lawson's *Negligence in the Civil Law* (Oxford University Press) contains a detailed examination of the Lex Aquilia and the adoption of its principles in modern legal systems. Lawson's *Roman Law Reader* (Oceana) contains a useful and interesting anthology collected from both ancient and modern writers.

Roman Legal Texts

F. de Zulueta, *Institutes of Gaius*, Vol. I (Oxford University Press) and J. A. C. Thomas, *Institutes of Justinian* (North Holland) contain the original texts of the *Institutes* and give side-by-side English translations.

PENGUIN  CLASSICS

THE DIGEST OF ROMAN LAW

ADVISORY EDITOR: BETTY RADICE

FLAVIUS PETRUS SABBATIUS IUSTINIANUS was Roman Emperor of the East, A.D. 527–65, having first ruled jointly with his elderly uncle the Emperor Justin from 518 to 527. He had a strong sense of his imperial rank and mission. In the East he held Persia in check by a war fought in Syria and Mesopotamia, 527–32, and by further campaigns from 540 onwards. In the Balkans he dealt successfully with a succession of threats from barbarian invaders. At home, his rule was shaken in 532 by the famous 'Nike' riots, which he finally quelled in blood. It was in the West, however, that Justinian's ambitions were made clear with his determination to reassert forcibly the majesty and control of the Empire. In campaigns fought in Africa and Italy through the great general Belisarius, he was able to largely recover the Western Empire by the year 540. Justinian's excessive financial administration resulted in the heavy indebtedness of the state. Nevertheless, as befitted his grand conception of this office, he built on a lavish scale; the Church of Hagia Sophia in Constantinople being his greatest monument. Vexed by the Monophysite heresy, he determined to impose peace on the Church and found a formula for unity at the Council of Chalcedon. His supreme achievement, however, was the great codification of Roman law (the *Digest*, *Institutes* and *Novellae*). His long reign ended in darkness, with storms gathering and the Empire ravaged by plague.

COLIN KOLBERT was educated in the Classics at Queen Elizabeth's, Barnet, and in the Law at St Catharine's College, Cambridge (where he completed his Ph.D.), and Lincoln's Inn (where he was called to the Bar). He has held university lectureships at Oxford, where he was Fellow and Tutor in Jurisprudence at St Peter's College, and at Cambridge, where he was Fellow, Tutor and Director of Studies at Magdalene College. His recent publications include works on English, Scots and Irish land law and African customary land tenures. He also writes on music. He is now a Circuit Judge and an Emeritus Fellow of Magdalene College, Cambridge.